Tippett and his Operas

by the same author

THE ARTS COUNCIL OF GREAT BRITAIN
STRAVINSKY: THE COMPOSER AND HIS WORKS
BENJAMIN BRITTEN: HIS LIFE AND OPERAS

TIPPETT
AND HIS OPERAS

ERIC WALTER WHITE

Barrie & Jenkins, London

Barrie & Jenkins Limited
3 Fitzroy Square, London W I P 6 J D

An imprint of the Hutchinson Publishing Group

London Melbourne Sydney Auckland
Wellington Johannesburg and agencies
throughout the world

First published 1979

© Eric Walter White 1979

Set in Monotype Garamond
by South Bucks Typesetters Ltd

Printed and bound in Great Britain by
William Clowes (Beccles) Limited
Beccles and London

ISBN 0 214 20573 8

This book is
affectionately dedicated to
Charles Osborne and Ken Thomson
with whom I have had so many
agreeable discussions
about these and
other operas

Contents

Illustrations

Acknowledgements

Some of this material has appeared previously elsewhere. Part of the Biographical Note is based on a chapter entitled 'A Biographical Sketch' which I contributed to *Michael Tippett*: *A Symposium on his 6oth Birthday*, edited by Ian Kemp (Faber & Faber, 1965); and another part on a 'Portrait' which I wrote for the *London Magazine*, also on the occasion of his 6oth birthday. Essays of mine on *The Midsummer Marriage* appeared in the *Adelphi*, 1955, on *King Priam* ('Tippett on Troy') in the *Western Daily Press*, 7 May 1962, on *The Knot Garden* ('Before the Curtain Rises . . .') in *Music Teacher*, October, November, December 1975 and January 1976, and on *The Ice Break* in *About the House* (The Magazine of the Friends of Covent Garden), spring 1977 and spring 1979. Thanks are due to the editors and publishers concerned, though it is only fair to emphasize that all this material has been extensively rewritten and enlarged for the present book.

I am indebted to Sir Michael Tippett for permission to quote from his correspondence with me and from his own published writings, including his opera librettos. At every stage in planning and writing this book I have had the kindest and most helpful collaboration from his publishers, Schott & Co. Ltd, London, and in particular from Mr Alan Woolgar. I am especially grateful to Mr Meirion Bowen for judicious advice generously given, and to Mrs Nest Cleverdon for help with the typing.

I

Biographical Note

'... simply the thing I am shall make me live'

Michael (Kemp) Tippett was born in a London nursing home on 2 January 1905.

His father, Henry William Tippett, was of Cornish stock and was born in 1858 just after the Crimean War. A Manchester liberal by conviction, he was trained as a lawyer and made sufficient money through the shrewd backing of various enterprises, including the Lyceum Theatre, London, to be able to retire from the legal profession at a comparatively early age. From him his son inherited his Celtic features and temperament.

His mother, Isabel Clementina Binny Kemp, came from Kent. An author in her own right, she had a pleasant singing voice and was in the habit of singing songs by ballad composers such as Roger Quilter. Her son acquired his early taste for music from her.

Late in 1905 the family, then consisting of the parents and two young boys, moved from Eastcote, Middlesex, to the small Suffolk village of Wetherden, between Bury St Edmunds and Stowmarket, where they stayed until 1919.

At an early stage it was arranged that the young Michael should have weekly piano lessons from the village teacher; and these continued until he went to public school. After a short period at Brookfield Preparatory School, Swanage, Dorset, he was sent to Fettes College, Edinburgh. After two wasted years in which he suffered from persecution, he was transferred to Stamford Grammar School, Lincolnshire. There his musical studies prospered under Mrs Tinkler, who had previously taught Malcolm Sargent; and one day he enjoyed an unexpected bonus when the English master, who was a gifted amateur musician, sang and played him some of the English folk songs collected and arranged by Cecil Sharp, and some of Dowland's lute songs then recently published. Writing about this more than fifty years later, the composer recalled with delight the profound impression this musical experience had made on his then 'totally untutored musical mind'.*

During the period immediately after the First World War, it was difficult for persons living in the provinces to hear much music of importance. Celebrity concerts reached only the larger provincial cities; festivals were few and far between; there was no wide choice of recorded music on the gramophone; and radio was in its infancy. So it was hardly surprising that an orchestral concert the schoolboy was allowed to attend at the De Montfort Hall, Leicester, should have delighted him. The conductor was the young Malcolm Sargent; and the programme included at least one contemporary work, namely Ravel's *Mother Goose* suite. The shock of this direct contact with symphonic music helped to confirm a feeling that had been growing in Tippett, that, come what might, he would devote the rest of his life to music in some form or other, but preferably by way of composition.

Because of financial difficulties, his parents decided to leave England in 1919 and live abroad. This meant that many of the schoolboy's holidays were spent visiting them in the south of France or Corsica, or in Florence. They were worried by his wish to take up music as a career; and in 1922 they consulted Malcolm Sargent, but were hardly reassured when he replied 'My advice to those about to become composers is (generally speaking) Don't!' Despite this discouragement, it was agreed that Michael should be sent to the Royal College of Music, where he studied composition under Charles Wood and C. H. Kitson, piano under Aubin Raymar, and conducting under Adrian Boult and Malcolm Sargent. He has left it on record that he found the training very 'Central European' in character.

My teacher, Charles Wood, had been taught by Stanford, who had been taught at Leipzig. The tradition was exactly that which trained Wagner. The stylistic and formal models were the German classics, the harmony was the central system built on thirds, and the counterpoint tied to this harmony (never, as is in some older English music, independently). This is a marvellous tradition of training in composition. But for the present day, as for the England of my student days, it is too narrow.†

*See 'A Personal view of music in England' by Michael Tippett from *Festschrift fur einen Verleger: Ludwig Strecker zum 90. Geburtstag*, B. Schott's Söhne, Mainz, 1973.
†*Ibid.*

This period was important, not only for his training as a music student, but also because of the opportunities he had for attending concerts and plays, reading books, and taking part in discussions about various subjects, including esthetics, ethics, politics, and psychology.

During his first summer in London, he rarely missed a night at the Proms; and his figure, dressed in white flannels and laden with miniature scores, became a familiar sight. His early piano studies had already familiarized him with Beethoven's piano sonatas; and he now became acquainted with the symphonies as conducted by Henry Wood, and a little later had a chance of hearing the Lener Quartet play all the string quartets. Although his musical tastes when they matured were to range widely – from Palestrina, Monteverdi, Purcell and Handel, to Bartok, Hindemith, Stravinsky and Ives – Beethoven was to remain his musical centre, a lodestar to which he knew he could always return.

He left college in 1928 with the degree of B Mus. He now had to decide how to direct his life. His resolution to dedicate himself to music was quite unshaken; but there were financial problems to be faced. For some years he tried to supplement his modest income by teaching. He taught French (not music) for two or three years at Hazlewood Preparatory School, Limpsfield, Surrey, where he became friendly with Christopher Fry, who happened to be the English master there; but he soon realized that teaching was an unsatisfactory compromise so far as he was concerned, and likely to prove a hindrance to his musical career. So he decided to drop it. He had recently been invited to become conductor of a newly formed concert and operatic society promoted by the Oxted and Limpsfield Players; and it was at Oxted, Surrey, in 1929 that he decided to build himself a small cottage, where he lived for the next twenty-two years:

Here he found the quiet he needed for thinking out his music. His life was almost a recluse's. Sometimes he ate at a neighbouring farm. More often he cooked for himself. In the morning he composed; in the afternoon went for a long walk, rain or shine; in the evening either worked with his choirs or wrote music again.*

With the aid of the local Oxted and Limpsfield Players, he was able to mount a number of operas at the Barn Theatre, Oxted, including

*Charles Reid, 'Michael Tippett: portrait of a twentieth-century composer', *Radio Times*, 13 February 1953.

Vaughan Williams's *The Shepherds of the Delectable Mountains*, Stanford's *The Travelling Companion*, and his own realization of the eighteenth-century ballad opera, *The Village Opera*. This he adapted, compressing and altering it so that the attempted elopement by night and by ladder was followed by a scene where the elopement was discovered. This scene he wrote afresh, both words and music, and it was through-composed for a small orchestra of solo woodwind, strings, harpsichord and piano. The production at the Barn Theatre, Oxted, in April 1929 received a favourable notice in *The Times*, whose critic wrote: 'The most successful scene was that of the elopement, where Mr Michael Tippett, who arranged and composed the music, showed a real sense of how to handle a dramatic situation in music.'

But progress was disappointingly slow where his other compositions were concerned. On 5 April 1930 David Moule Evans conducted a concert of his recent works at the Barn Theatre; and the composer, who was present, was so dissatisfied by what he heard that he decided to scrap most of what he had written to date. The Oxted programme included a Concerto in D for flutes, oboe, horns and strings in four movements, a String Quartet in F in five movements, and a Psalm in C (a setting of *The Gateway* by Christopher Fry) for chorus and orchestra. The score of the Concerto in D was subsequently destroyed. The String Quartet and the Psalm were never published, but the scores remained in the composer's collection.

This concert showed Tippett that his technique was still dangerously immature. With characteristic courage, he made up his mind that the proper remedy was to go back to school and, later that year, made arrangements through the Royal College of Music to work as a private pupil of R. O. Morris. A rigorous course of fugue that lasted for about eighteen months braced him for a fresh attempt at composition. Two of the works that followed, namely a Symphony in B flat (written 1933-4, revised 1935) and *A Song of Liberty*, a choral setting dated May Day 1937 of words by William Blake from *The Marriage of Heaven and Hell*, were also discarded as being unsatisfactory; but the first String Quartet (original version 1935) was the first work to reach his exacting standards and to be included in the definitive canon of his compositions.

In the early 1930s life in England was poisoned by the canker of the Great Depression; and this naturally had a strong effect on a composer who felt as strongly 'committed' as the young Tippett. In 1932 he was invited to take charge of music at work camps near

Boosbeck, a small mining village in the Cleveland district of north Yorkshire. The camps, initiated by Rolf Gardiner, were designed to help unemployed ironstone miners gain some independence and solvency by encouraging the growth of a land economy and of a local culture. At Boosbeck Tippett directed performances with local people taking part in *The Beggar's Opera* (1932) and his own folk-song opera (so far unpublished) *Robin Hood* (1933).

He was horrified by the appearance of the undernourished children of the unemployed in that part of Yorkshire and felt ashamed of himself when he returned to the well-fed south, where more work of social importance awaited him.

In 1932 he was appointed conductor of the South London Orchestra of unemployed professional musicians, which rehearsed regularly at Morley College and gave concerts, generally of popular classics, in LCC schools and in churches, settlements, hospitals and parks. The players – about forty-five in all – were recruited mainly from the ranks of instrumentalists who had lost their jobs in cinema bands on the arrival of the sound film; and a number of eminent artists, including Harriet Cohen, Myra Hess, Phyllis Sellick, Cyril Smith, and Solomon, gave their services at various concerts that were run for the benefit of the players. In addition, Tippett wrote and arranged music for special performances given by school children under the auspices of the Royal Arsenal Co-operative Society's education department at Abbey Wood near Woolwich and at New Malden. He became involved in this work through his friendship with Alan Bush and Francesca Allinson, both conductors of choirs associated with the working-class movement.

At this period Tippett was a Trotsky sympathizer, though not a member of any Trotskyite party. He joined the Communist Party for a few months in 1935, but left when he realized he would not succeed in converting his party branch to Trotskyism. His active interest in Trotskyism began to wane when he saw that left-wing politics were unable to offer any answer to the barbarities of Nazism or Communism; and from the beginning of the Second World War he threw in his lot with the Peace Pledge Union, which had been founded by the Rev. Dick Sheppard in 1935.*

The first performance of String Quartet no. 1 (subsequently

---

*This paragraph is based on information supplied by Ian Kemp for the Chronology printed in the Michael Tippett Exhibition Catalogue (Schott, 1977).

revised in 1943 when a new first movement replaced the original first and second movements) was given by the Brosa Quartet at a Lemare Concert at the Mercury Theatre, London, in December 1935. It was followed by a Sonata for Piano (written in 1936–7; revised in 1942 and 1954) first performed by Phyllis Sellick at Queen Mary Hall, London, in November 1938, and a Concerto for Double String Orchestra (1938–9) first performed by the South London Orchestra, conducted by the composer at Morley College, London, in April 1940.

During the period of Munich and the months immediately preceding the outbreak of war, Tippett felt impelled to write something that would make an impassioned protest against the horrors of the Nazi menace that was building up in Germany. At first he was not clear whether the work ought to be an opera or an oratorio; but when Herschel Grynsban, a young Polish Jew aged seventeen, goaded to desperation by Nazi persecution, shot the German diplomat, von Rath, at the German legation in Paris, thereby causing a savage pogrom of the Jews in central Europe, he realized that what he needed was the libretto for an oratorio based on a similar contemporary situation. His first idea was that it should be written by a poet: so he approached T. S. Eliot, whose verse play, *The Family Reunion*, had shown with what intensity a myth could be presented in contemporary terms, and enquired whether he would be prepared to collaborate in a work which (in Tippett's own words) would show how 'an outcast is thrown up for one moment by the forces of history and by his personal fate as protagonist opposite the tyrant, the man of destiny'. Eliot asked if he might see a rough draft of the sort of thing required;* and when that was forthcoming, his comment was that the composer had virtually completed the job himself. So Tippett revised his own rough draft and used it as basis for the libretto of *A Child of Our Time*. He began the composition on 5 September 1939, just two days after the outbreak of war.

So far no interest had been expressed by any British firm in the possibility of publishing his music. In fact, his most recent work, the Concerto for Double String Orchestra, had been rejected for performance by the British Broadcasting Corporation, rejected for performance by the British section of the ISCM, and rejected for

---

*This draft has been reprinted in *Music of the Angels*, edited by Meirion Bowen (Ernst Eulenburg, 1979).

publication 'by very well-known English publishers of the time'.*
Early in 1939 the BBC presented a concert performance of Paul
Hindemith's *Mathis der Maler* (15 March). Some years later Tippett
recalled the occasion:

At the last-named [performance], in the old London Queens Hall (destroyed
in the subsequent fratricidal war), a friend persuaded me to overcome my
shyness and to be introduced, in one of the intervals, to a tall distinguished
figure in full evening dress, talking to friends in the foyer. This was Willi
Strecker, of Schott's, Mainz, one of the most well-loved, unforgotten, greatly
cultured figures of European music publishing. I can recall this meeting as
though it was only yesterday. He too sensed my shyness and then, giving
me his professional card, he exacted a promise that I would send him a copy,
not only of pieces that I thought good and publishable, but of everything
right back to juvenilia, so that he could make a reasonable assessment of
what the composer was altogether.†

The reply that the London firm received from Mainz just after the
outbreak of war stated that as a first step Schott's Söhne, Mainz, were
prepared to publish two works. These were the Concerto for Double
String Orchestra and the Piano Sonata no. 1. At that moment it was
clear there would be no speedy end to the war, so in the event Tippett's
music was published by Schott & Co. Ltd, London, instead of
Schott's Söhne, Mainz. The first items to appear in print (in 1942)
were the Piano Sonata and the Fantasia on a Theme of Handel for
Piano and Orchestra (written 1939–41). *A Child of Our Time* (1939–41)
followed in 1944, and the Concerto for Double String Orchestra in
1946.

The war affected Tippett in a number of ways. First of all, his work
with the Royal Arsenal Co-operative Society's choirs came to an end,
and to replace the income he lost thereby he reverted to his old role
of schoolmaster and taught classics for a while at Hazelwood. And
then his bonds with Morley College were strengthened. On 15
October 1940 the building was hit and almost completely destroyed
by a high-explosive bomb; but arrangements were promptly made
for music classes to continue in a neighbouring school. At this
juncture Tippett was invited by Eva Hubback, the principal, to
become director of music at the college in succession to Arnold
Foster. His intrepid enthusiasm triumphantly overcame the diffi-

*Tippett, 'A personal view of music in England'.
†*Ibid.*

culties and discouragements of that wartime period; and by the beginning of the 1941–2 season he had built up the choir from eight voices to thirty. In the latter part of 1942 he met Benjamin Britten and Peter Pears, who had just returned to England after a three-year stay in North America and were now appearing at special wartime concerts organised by CEMA (the Council for the Encouragement of Music and the Arts). Tippett was about to perform one of Purcell's verse anthems, 'My Beloved Spake', at Morley, when Walter Bergmann suggested Peter Pears would be ideal as the tenor soloist. Britten accompanied Pears to the rehearsal; and a friendship between the three musicians was quickly struck up. The result was that in January 1943 Tippett composed a cantata – *Boyhood's End* – on a text by W. H. Hudson for tenor and piano, which he dedicated to Pears and Britten, and early that summer they gave the first performance of it in the Holst Room at Morley College.

Shortly after the outbreak of war Tippett had applied for provisional registration as a conscientious objector. His case was not heard by the London tribunal until 1942, when he was directed to non-combatant military duties. On appeal he was given conditional registration, provided he undertook some approved form of work such as agricultural labour, hospital portering, and so on. He constantly refused to accept the jobs offered because of his conviction that music was the field in which he could best serve the community; and he was eventually brought to trial at Oxted Police Court on the charge of failing to comply with the conditions of his exemption. Dr Ralph Vaughan Williams was called for the defence and testified as follows:

I think Tippett's pacifist views entirely wrong, but I respect him very much for holding them so firmly. I think his compositions are very remarkable and form a distinct national asset, and will increase the prestige of this country in the world. As regards his teachings at Morley College, it is distinctly work of national importance to create a musical atmosphere at the College and elsewhere. We know music is forming a great part in national life now; more since the war than ever before, and everyone able to help on with that work is doing work of national importance.

Despite this eloquent plea, Tippett was sentenced (on 21 June 1943) to three months imprisonment in Wormwood Scrubs.

He had finished the composition of *A Child of Our Time* just before serving this sentence. The words of the air that the Boy sings in his prison cell –

'My dreams are all shattered in a ghastly reality.
The wild beating of my heart is stilled, day by day.
Earth and sky are not for those in prison.'

might have been thought to apply to the composer's own situation. But no. Whatever the rights or wrongs of his individual case might be, there was nothing depressed in his bearing or defeatist about his attitude to life. He had shown that he had the courage to stick to his opinions; and this, if anything, increased his self-confidence as a man dedicated to music and the respect felt for him by his friends and fellow-musicians. '. . . simply the thing I am shall make me live.' Perhaps the most pregnant comment on this episode was made by his mother some years later when she was being congratulated by a friend on her son's being awarded a CBE in the honours list. When the friend added that she must feel very proud of him, she replied: 'My proudest moment was the day he went to prison!'*

He had one unexpected pleasure while he was in jail. Peter Pears and Benjamin Britten visited Wormwood Scrubs as part of one of their regular CEMA concert tours and were accompanied by John Amis, who has described the occasion as follows:

The authorities were bamboozled into thinking that the music to be performed was so complicated that it required the expert services of Michael on the platform to help me turn over the pages for Britten. (I had got into the prison only for that purpose.)†

As soon as he was out of jail, Tippett took up his work where he had left it off and busied himself at Morley College with a series of monthly chamber concerts featuring music by Purcell, Gibbons, Dowland, Monteverdi, Stravinsky, Hindemith, and Britten, together with some of his own compositions. About this time, Britten, who was becoming interested in Tippett's music, asked what large-scale works he had written other than those already published by Schott's. After considering the matter, Tippett remembered *A Child of Our Time*, the score of which had been finished in 1941 but, on the advice of Walter Goehr, put away in a drawer for the time being. Britten was enthusiastic about the oratorio and urged Tippett to plan an early performance despite the difficulties of wartime conditions. This was

*See Sybil Morrison's contribution to *Michael Tippett: a A Symposium on his 60th birthday*, edited by Ian Kemp (Faber & Faber, 1965).

†From 'Wartime Melody' by John Amis, in *Michael Tippett: A Symposium on his 60th Birthday*.

given at the Adelphi Theatre, London, on 19 March 1944 with Walter Goehr conducting the London Philharmonic Orchestra, the London Region Civil Defence and Morley College Choirs, and Joan Cross, Margaret McArthur, Peter Pears, and Roderick Lloyd as the four soloists.

Owing mainly to the difficulties of rehearsing an important new work in wartime conditions, this performance was not an exemplary one; but subsequent performances in England began to reveal the true strength and originality of the work, and it was soon realized that it exercised a strong appeal abroad. For instance, the 1947 performance at Arnhem was a deeply moving occasion. The Dutch performers and audience felt convinced that such a work could have been written only by someone who had experienced the same sufferings as themselves; and the music acted as a catalyst, releasing deep heart-felt emotions that had been pent up during the dark years of the occupation. In a different context, similarly strong and valid emotions were released by a performance in Zambia about a quarter of a century later.

When the war ended, Tippett and Goehr embarked on a more ambitious policy of concert promotion. The Morley College Concerts Society was set up with financial backing from the Arts Council of Great Britain (formerly CEMA), and several old and new works of considerable novelty and interest were presented. In 1946 *A Child of Our Time* was revived (19 March), and on 14 May Monteverdi's *Vespers* of 1610, which had never been played in Great Britain before, was performed at the Central Hall, Westminster, and made a very deep impression on the public. Contemporary works included the first concert performance in Great Britain of Stravinsky's *Les Noces*, the world première of Matyas Seiber's *Ulysses*, and the first London performance of Tippett's Symphony no. 1 (1944–5). A few years later, as part of the London Season of the Arts in the Festival of Britain, 1951, the society revived Monteverdi's *Vespers* and Tippett's *A Child of Our Time* and gave the first London performance of Carl Orff's *Carmina Burana*, and the first European performance of Stravinsky's *Babel*.

After these Festival of Britain concerts, Tippett resigned as director of music at Morley College and was succeeded by Peter Racine Fricker, who had been a member of the Morley choir for some years, first as a singer, then as rehearsal pianist and assistant conductor. Towards the end of 1952 Tippett accepted an invitation to join

Barbara Hepworth and Priaulx Rainier in assuming responsibility for the artistic direction of the St Ives (Cornwall) Festival of the Arts in the summer of 1953. He composed two trumpet Fanfares (nos. 2 and 3) specially for that occasion.

By now Schott's had more or less caught up with publishing the backlog of his compositions; and as a consequence there were more frequent performances of his music. The voices of two well-informed critics were also heard at a comparatively early date, drawing attention to the originality of his music in terms of shrewd understanding and discriminating praise. During the latter part of the war, William Glock, then music critic of *The Observer*, paid special attention to Tippett's new compositions and seemed to regard him and Britten (who was just over eight years his junior) as the two outstanding British composers of their generation. Edward Sackville-West also grouped them together in an extended study that he wrote for *Horizon*. While making a comparative assessment of the two composers, he referred to Tippett's music in the following terms:

It has none of the vivid colour, the immediate dramatic effectiveness, the winning sensuous beauty, of Britten's best work. Its strength is that of consistency and rational construction informed by an emotional and intransigent nature.*

The example of Britten was of crucial importance at that moment. The post-war success of his first opera *Peter Grimes* did much to direct the attention of British composers to the importance of opera as a medium. Tippett heard it when it was first produced at Sadler's Wells Theatre in the summer of 1945 – and also in Budapest when he visited Hungary late in 1948 at the time of the Bartok Festival. In some ways *A Child of Our Time* had been a step in the direction of opera. In a programme note he drafted for one of the oratorio's early performances, he wrote:

Because an oratorio, like an opera, has a story and ideas, these forms are impure musically as compared with symphonies and sonatas. But the impurity can also become the cause that we are moved the more deeply, moved beyond analysis or consciousness of that which moves us.

His Symphony no. 1 was composed towards the end of the war and received its first performance by the Liverpool Philharmonic Orchestra conducted by Malcolm Sargent at the Philharmonic Hall, Liver-

*Edward Sackville-West, 'Music: some aspects of the contemporary problem', *Horizon*, June–July–August 1944.

pool, in November 1945. After composing it he felt the need to embark on an opera that would form a pendant to his oratorio and provide an answer to its 'music from the dark world'. A moment of intense personal vision gave him the conviction that he had become 'the instrument of some collective imaginative experience', and profiting by this feeling of excitement, he decided to invent his own fable and become his own librettist. A full account of his struggle to plan the action and write the words and music of this important opera is to be found in his notebooks as reprinted in *Music of the Angels* and in his letters addressed to me during the period 1948–55 as printed later in this book.

Immediately after the end of the war, the Arts Council of Great Britain was set up under Royal Charter; and one of its first steps was to create advisory panels for music, drama, and the visual arts. Tippett was appointed to the music panel in July 1945 and served until December 1949. That meant that he became conversant not only with the Council's evolving policy for helping large and small orchestras, and music societies of various kinds, but also with the early moves for establishing opera on a permanent basis, and in particular for subsidising the work of the Royal Opera House (Covent Garden) and Sadler's Wells with their various dependent opera and ballet companies. Although post-war Covent Garden had no settled policy governing the presentation of English operas as such, *The Olympians* by Arthur Bliss had been given there in 1949. *The Pilgrim's Progress* by Vaughan Williams and *Billy Budd* by Britten were specially mounted during the Festival of Britain year (1951). Britten's *Gloriana* followed in the coronation summer of 1953. William Walton's *Troilus and Cressida* and Tippett's *The Midsummer Marriage* were both accepted for production in the 1954–5 season.

The first performance of *The Midsummer Marriage* took place at Covent Garden on 27 January 1955, in the month of the composer's fiftieth birthday. The conductor was John Pritchard. At first the public was uncertain what to make of it, particularly as the libretto was thought to be confusing in parts and obscure; and the mixed notices showed that some of the critics had lost their nerve. But gradually the music became recognised for its great beauty and power; and it won the support of a growing band of enthusiasts, whose numbers were considerably increased when in 1971 the work was recorded under the direction of Colin Davis with the soloists, chorus and orchestra of the Royal Opera House.

With the completion of *The Midsummer Marriage* Tippett had shown himself capable of tackling all the major musical forms – opera, oratorio, symphony, concerto, string quartet, sonata, and so on. Of these it now became evident that the operas took the longest time to gestate and compose. He seemed to need about three years (part-time) in which to meditate on the collective experience to be developed and presented operatically, and in which to draft the libretto; a further three years (virtually whole-time) for the composition of the score (about an act a year); and another year (part-time) in which to prepare the material for production. In other words, the process implied a seven-year cycle, which was sufficiently elastic to allow other forms of composition to be slotted in as well. Indeed, it might be thought that the prolonged three-year stint needed for the composition of each opera score stimulated his appetite for writing other forms of music; and there must have been moments when it occurred to him that some of the 'impure' music he was composing for one of his operas might be capable of 'purer' treatment at some other time in the context of symphonic form. In any case it is worth mentioning that the four Ritual Dances that are featured in Acts II and III of *The Midsummer Marriage* made a separate reputation for themselves quite early on as a concert suite with optional chorus. In this form they were first performed by the Basel Kammerorchestra conducted by Paul Sacher in Basel in February 1953.

In 1951, after living for twenty-two years in Oxted, Surrey, Tippett moved to Tidebrook Manor, Wadhurst, Sussex. The first music he composed in his new home was Act III of *The Midsummer Marriage*.

The completion of this opera released a number of other important works – including the Fantasia Concertante on a Theme of Corelli for string orchestra (1953), the Divertimento on 'Sellinger's Round' for chamber orchestra (1953–4), the Sonata for Four Horns (1955) and particularly the Concerto for Piano and Orchestra (1953–5), the idiom of which was particularly close to that of the opera.

To celebrate his fiftieth birthday in 1955, a concert was given in the Holst Room at Morley College with a programme that included Margaret Kitchin playing the Sonata for Piano no. 1, *Boyhood's End* performed by Peter Pears and Benjamin Britten, and the String Quartet no. 1 played by the Aeolian Quartet.

He now began to receive a steady stream of commissions from individuals and institutions, of which the BBC was possibly the most important.

His first BBC commission came in 1944, when he was asked to compose 'The Weeping Babe', a motet for soprano solo and unaccompanied chorus (SATB) to a poem by Edith Sitwell for a radio programme entitled *Poets' Christmas*. In 1948 the corporation invited him to write a suite for the birthday of Prince Charles (Suite in D) which was first performed by the BBC Symphony Orchestra conducted by Sir Adrian Boult in November 1948. His Symphony no. 2 (1956–7) was also the result of a BBC commission and was also first performed by the BBC Symphony Orchestra conducted by Sir Adrian Boult at the Royal Festival Hall, February 1958. (This was the occasion on which the orchestra broke down shortly after the start of the first movement, and Sir Adrian, turning to the audience, said with characteristic chivalry, 'Ladies and gentlemen – entirely *my* fault I'm afraid!' and started the movement over again.) The fortieth anniversary of the corporation in 1962 was commemorated by a specially commissioned work, Praeludium for Brass, Bells and Percussion, first performed by the BBC Symphony Orchestra under Antal Dorati at the Royal Festival Hall, November 1962. A few years later *The Vision of Saint Augustine* (1963–5) for baritone solo, chorus and orchestra was commissioned for a performance at the Royal Festival Hall with Dietrich Fischer-Dieskau as soloist and the composer conducting the BBC Symphony Orchestra, January 1966. Later in 1966 the BBC West Region commissioned 'Severn Bridge Variation no. 6 *Braint*' from Tippett as part of a composite work to commemorate the first birthday of the BBC Training Orchestra, its first visit to Wales, and the opening of the Severn Bridge. An interesting radio programme in which he was involved was *Words for Music Perhaps*, where he provided incidental music for speaking voices and a chamber ensemble to a sequence of poems by W. B. Yeats (first broadcast, June 1960).

He was also engaged to give a number of broadcast talks, generally for the Third Programme. A particularly important series of three formed part of a prolonged obituary tribute to Arnold Schoenberg in 1952. A few years later, he contributed a striking series of articles on the genesis of *The Midsummer Marriage* to *The Observer*. These together with other broadcasts, articles and papers were collected in *Moving into Aquarius*,* a book which revealed the author's passionate preoccupation with 'what sort of world we live in and how we may

---

*Routledge & Kegan Paul, 1959, revised and enlarged edition, Paladin, 1974.

behave in it', and the importance of discovering and maintaining the right sort of personal relationships. His impact as a public figure was extended later on when he began to take part in television broadcasts, his appearance in the Monitor film made in 1963 to commemorate Britten's fiftieth birthday being particularly striking.

Tippett showed his willingness to be involved in music for young people when in 1957 he accepted a commission from the parent of one of the girls at Badminton School, Bristol, to compose a piece to commemorate the centenary in 1958 of the school's foundation. He chose a text by Christopher Fry entitled *Crown of the Year*, which dealt lyrically with four great queens – Elizabeth I, Anne, Victoria, and Elizabeth II. The four-part division meant that the composer was able to gear the composition to the four seasons of the year as well as the reigns of the four queens, and each of the four movements contained an instrumental prelude and choral refrain as well as a special number written for chorus or for solo voice or voices. It was remarkable to discover how easily the young girls of Badminton School embraced Tippett's contemporary idiom, whether singing in the choir or playing in the band. Recalling the occasion twenty years later in a letter dated June 1978, Judith Catty (*née* Last) wrote:

What a challenge it was! We had been brought up on a diet of madrigals, folk songs, and the traditional choral works; and here was something totally different. From the first we were aware of and involved in the vitality, the joy, and the musicality. There had been ominous warnings about the difficulty of the music; but at no time do I remember sweat or despair in the preparation. And it was no false modesty that made us shrug our shoulders when the adults in the audience commented that we were performing without scores. We had been well drilled, of course; but I remember the tingle of excitement each time I heard the brilliant piano part and we began singing. And this brilliance, this excitement and vivacity were with us every time.

The composer found it a rewarding experience too. In a letter to me he wrote:

I have never doubted that young people eventually respond to quality in music, if that is there, despite the initial problem of a new (and unknown) style. Even matters of technical difficulty resolve themselves to a large extent in the satisfaction of playing together the notes the composer imagined.*

*Quoted from 'Crown of the year' by Eric Walter White, in *Michael Tippett: A Symposium on his Sixtieth Birthday*.

The year 1959 marked the tercentenary of Henry Purcell's birth. Tippett's interest in Purcell and his music had not declined since his Morley College days; but now he found he had fewer opportunities of taking part in actual performances. Over the years, however, he and Walter Bergmann had collaborated in editing the 'Ode for St Cecilia's Day' (1692), the 'Ode for the Birthday of Queen Mary' (1694), and the Golden Sonata, together with about twenty songs and duets, all published by Schott's. He now accepted an invitation. from Imogen Holst to contribute something to a collection of essays on Purcell's music that she was editing and wrote 'Our sense of continuity in English drama and music',* in which he used the examples of Purcell and Shakespeare to illustrate what he thought was the proper correlation of verse drama and opera.

In the summer of 1957 he was offered a commission by the Koussevitzky Music Foundation to write a choral and orchestral piece of about twenty to thirty minutes' duration. He accepted; but when he came to tackle the new composition, he found it had changed direction, and he was beginning to think of it in operatic terms. Eventually a full-scale new opera resulted from the Gulbenkian-commission. After discussing various points of theatrical technique with Peter Brook, who about ten years previously had been appointed director of productions to the Covent Garden Opera Company, he came to the conclusion that on this occasion he would use a public rather than a private myth as the basis of his plot, and accordingly chose a number of scenes from the *Iliad* dealing with the story of Priam and his sons Hector and Paris and illustrating problems arising from the necessity of choice. What was implicit, though not actually stated, was that their choice was directed, not by free-will, but by necessity itself – they made their choices, not because they wanted to, but because they had to. Once again he decided to be his own librettist. The composition of the score of *King Priam* took three years (1958–61). It seemed appropriate that the first performance of the new opera should have been given by the Covent Garden Opera Company conducted by John Pritchard at the Coventry Theatre, Coventry, on 29 May 1962 as part of the festival held to celebrate the rededication of St Michael's Cathedral, since a few years previously some of Tippett's music had been chosen to accompany a documentary film featuring the destruction of the old cathedral as a result of the bombing

*Henry Purcell, 1659–1695: Essays on His Music, edited by Imogen Holst (Oxford University Press, 1959).

raids during the last war, and Sir Basil Spence's plans for building a new one.

As had been the case with *The Midsummer Marriage*, the completion of the new opera left the way open for the composition of a number of related works, all of which showed a close affinity with its stark and rugged style – particularly the Sonata no. 2 for Piano (1962) and the Concerto for Orchestra (1962–3). The latter was commissioned for the Edinburgh Festival of 1963 and dedicated to Benjamin Britten 'with affection and admiration in the year of his fiftieth birthday'. In addition there were two parerga of special interest – *Songs for Achilles* (1961) consisting of a set of three songs for tenor and guitar, the first ('In the Tent') being the song sung by Achilles in the second scene of Act II of the opera, the other two ('Across the Plain' and 'By the Sea') being freshly composed to new texts written by the composer; and a Prelude, Recitative and Aria for flute, oboe and piano or harpsichord (1963), which is a transcription of the third interlude in Act III, with the vocal part of Hermes rearranged for oboe.

Shortly before the first performance of *King Priam*, Tippett moved (in 1960) from Wadhurst to a house on the Methuen estate at Corsham, Wiltshire. Here he remained until 1970, when he moved only a short distance away to a new house on the edge of the Marlborough Downs.

In 1962 he accepted an invitation to provide incidental music for a production of *The Tempest* at the Old Vic, London. The first numbers to be written were the three *Songs for Ariel*. These were published (in 1962) for voice and piano (or harpsichord), and later they appeared in an instrumental arrangement for flute/piccolo, clarinet, horn, and percussion *ad lib.* (bells, bass drum, and harpsichord). They seem to have had a kind of seminal influence on some of his later works. For instance, motifs from them were incorporated into *The Knot Garden* (1966–70) and *Songs for Dov* (1970). Apart from the *Songs for Ariel*, this incidental music to *The Tempest* has remained and is likely to remain unpublished, though in 1964 John Lambert arranged a score from it for a ballet presented by the London Dance Theatre with choreography by Andrée Howard to mark the Shakespeare Quatercentenary.

1965 was the year of his sixtieth birthday. A special present (received the previous year) was the dedication of Britten's parable for church performance, *Curlew River*. Among various tributes received in 1965 was a symposium in Festschrift style edited by Ian Kemp and published by Faber & Faber, containing a biographical sketch followed by a collection of tributes and reminiscences written by friends and collaborators, and a number of analytical essays on the main aspects of his compositions to date. A special concert was held on 2 January 1965 at the Emma Cons Hall, Morley College, with a programme that included String Quartet no. 1, the Sonata for four Horns, the *Songs for Ariel*, *Boyhood's End*, and *Crown of the Year*.

His next important work was *The Vision of St Augustine*, which some people may look on as the peak of his creative effort. The parental dedication – *matri, patrisque in memoriam* – is directed equally to the living and the dead. The work is not an oratorio and so does not qualify for treatment here on the same lines as *A Child of Our Time*. It is in fact a kind of transcendental canticle for baritone solo, chorus and orchestra. In the preface to the vocal score, Tippett specifically refers to two of Augustine's visions:

In his twenties Augustine went first to work in Rome and then in Milan. . . . In a garden near Milan, with Alypius his dearest friend, at thirty-three years of age, he had his first vision . . . of a child singing. . . . Some months later he decided to return with his mother to Africa. They travelled overland to Ostia, the port of Rome, and rested there before the sea voyage. Here, five days before Monica's death, Augustine had a second vision, which Monica shared – of Eternity.

As the attempt to express these visions and explore the idea of eternity in musical terms suffered from the limitations set by the inexpressible, the composer had recourse to the use of glossolalia in his Latin text, namely melismata consisting only of vowel sounds that transcend the common business of meaning. The first performance of this magnificent work was given by the BBC Symphony Orchestra conducted by the composer at the Royal Festival Hall in January 1966 with Dietrich Fischer-Dieskau as the soloist.

During the immediate post-war years, Stewart Mason, Director of Education for Leicestershire, had initiated an important art service for the schools in his county. Having persuaded the local education authority to set aside a comparatively modest annual sum of money for the visual arts, which was used to buy pictures and pieces of sculpture mainly by contemporary artists and to build up a collection from which loans could be made to the local schools, he now got them to extend this service to music by encouraging the formation of a Leicestershire Schools Symphony Orchestra. When Tippett was told about this experiment, he expressed interest and agreed to become a patron. In 1965 the orchestra visited him at Corsham; and, hearing the players sing *Non nobis* as a grace, he decided to make an orchestral version of it for them. Shortly afterwards it occurred to him that the instrumental *Non nobis* could become the epilogue to a new composition, or suite for orchestra, in several movements, and he added a prologue based on 'Sumer is icumen in'. In 1967 he accompanied the orchestra on a tour to Germany and conducted it at a concert in the Philharmonie, Berlin, where the programme included Hindemith's *Sinfonische Metamorphosen Carl Maria von Weber'scher Themen*, Ives's *Putnam's Camp*, Copland's *Quiet City*, and Gershwin's *Rhapsody in Blue*. He continued to work on this Suite for Orchestra, which grew by the accretion of further movements for orchestra and chorus. *The Shires Suite*, as it came to be called, was written over a period of six years and when completed consisted of:

Prologue for chorus and orchestra (1965)
Interlude 1 for orchestra (1970)
Cantata for chorus and orchestra (1970)
Interlude 2 for orchestra (1969)
Epilogue for chorus and orchestra (1965)

The first complete performance by the Schola Cantorum of Oxford and the Leicestershire Schools Symphony Orchestra was given at the Cheltenham Festival, July 1970, with the composer conducting.

From 1966 onwards a great deal of Tippett's time was taken up with planning, drafting and composing *The Knot Garden*. By 1969 not only had he completed the opera, but he also knew that the strophic song for Dov, which ended the second act, was going to be the cue for a further two songs which would complete a special song cycle for tenor and orchestra. The composition of *Songs for Dov* was completed early enough for the first performance to be given in Cardiff in October 1970 with Gerald English as the soloist and the composer conducting the London Sinfonietta. This was just two months before the first performance of *The Knot Garden* under the musical direction of Colin Davis at the Royal Opera House, Covent Garden (2 December 1970).

Since 1960, when he had moved from Wadhurst to Corsham, Tippett had become increasingly involved in the musical life of the South West. In 1969 he was appointed artistic director of the Bath Festival and held this post until 1974. This was the first time he had been publicly associated with a festival since the St Ives experiment of 1953. The Bath Festival programmes for these six years contained a number of items reflecting the director's special tastes, including an uncut performance (at the Colston Hall, Bristol) of Beethoven's music to *Egmont*. Tippett's new Piano Sonata no. 3, which had been commissioned by Paul Crossley, had its first performance at the 1973 Festival (26 May).

After the war, as performances of his music multiplied abroad, he found himself travelling frequently to Europe. After its London premiere, *A Child of Our Time* was played in Brussels, Hamburg, Arnhem, Budapest and Lausanne. The first European performance of the Concerto for Double String Orchestra was given by Schmidt-Isserstedt as part of the Frankfürter Woche für neue Musik in the summer of 1949. And *King Priam* was the first of Tippett's operas to be performed abroad when on 27 January 1963 the Badisches Staatstheater in Karlsruhe gave it in a German translation by Walter Bergmann. *The Midsummer Marriage* had to wait a further ten years for its first German production, also at the Badisches Staatstheater, Karlsruhe, under the musical direction of Arthur Grüber (29 September 1973).

While Tippett's music was gradually becoming known in Europe, interest in it was growing steadily in North America. A revealing comment was made by Aaron Copland in his contribution to the symposium published on Tippett's sixtieth birthday:

It is no problem at all for an American to like and empathize with Michael Tippett. ... I can remember remarking to myself, when I first met him, how very American his personality seemed. ... Something outgoing, something spirited and unabashed and almost boyishly enthusiastic makes him cousin to his American counterpart.

Copland had heard the Concerto for Double String Orchestra by accident and had thought it was a piece of American music with its liberal use of syncopated rhythms, cross-accents, and asymmetrical grouping of quavers.

In 1965 Tippett was invited to the Aspen Festival as composer in residence. This was his first visit to North America and, in the words of his friend Meirion Bowen, he felt

as if he had arrived in his own private Mayflower. Aspen was not New England, but it was his first contact with a polyglot culture that made a deep impression on him. He has responded equally, ever since, to the extra-ordinary contrasts provided by Spanish America and the Indians, the curious culture of the Pacific coast cities; the different races and creeds; the sky-scrapers of New York and Chicago; and the natural landscapes produced by erosion of red rock and sandstone in Monument Valley, Utah.*

After this initial visit he returned frequently, sometimes to conduct orchestras, sometimes to attend performances. For instance, in April 1968 he filled in at short notice for Igor Stravinsky and conducted the St Louis Symphony in his own Concerto for Orchestra. Early in 1974 he attended the first performance in North America of his Third Symphony (1970–2) given by the Boston Symphony Orchestra under Colin Davis in Boston and New York. Advantage was taken of his presence in Boston to mount a 'Sir Michael Tippett Festival' at Tufts University on 13 February 1974, the programme of which included his 'Fanfare for the Four Corners' (*i.e.* Fanfare no. 2), the *Songs for Achilles*, the *Songs for Ariel*, the Piano Sonata no. 2, the Fanfare for Brass (i.e. Fanfare no. 1, 1943) and the Sonata for Four Horns.

Mention of Stravinsky reminds one that after the maestro's death on 6 April 1971, his publishers, Boosey & Hawkes, invited a number of composers to write a short canon or epitaph by way of homage, and these contributions were printed in the Boosey & Hawkes house magazine, *Tempo*. Tippett's was a miniature six-bar piece for flute, clarinet, and string quartet entitled *In Memoriam Magistri*. It was first performed by the London Sinfonietta in a programme that included some of the other pieces of homage at St John's, Smith Square, London, in June 1972.

For some time the Library of Northwestern University, Evanston, Illinois, had shown interest in building up a collection of contem-porary music manuscripts. They had recently acquired the valuable Moldenhauer Archive, which it was intended should be made avail-able, not only for research and study, but for performance as well. I happened to be in touch with Don L. Roberts, the Head Music Librarian, who asked me if there was a chance of Northwestern acquiring the manuscript of one of Tippett's operas. At that time most of Tippett's compositions existed in two manuscript versions – a preliminary 'rough' score in pencil, and a final 'fair' copy in ink. I

*From 'America' by Meirion Bowen, reprinted in the Michael Tippett Exhibition Catalogue.

knew that the manuscript scores of *The Midsummer Marriage* and *King Priam* were not available: but I agreed to enquire about *The Knot Garden* and discovered the composer was prepared to sell the 'pencil' copy, together with one or two notebooks which he had used for roughing out the musical settings for various words and phrases in the libretto. All that remained was to agree a price.

Don Roberts happened to be coming over to London in the near future, so I arranged a meeting at a restaurant in Soho. This worked out extremely well. Recalling it some months later, Don Roberts said:

It happened that Michael and I had both stayed in the same dinky little hotel when we were visiting the Hopi Indian reservation in King's Canyon, Arizona. We hit it off immediately and not only did Northwestern get permission to acquire the original manuscript, but we began talking about the possibility of the American premiere of the work being staged at Northwestern.*

Accordingly in December 1972, Don Roberts and two of his colleagues – Robert Gay, director of the opera theatre, and Sam Ball, head of design in the theatre department – came over to London to familiarize themselves with the Peter Hall production, which had just been revived at Covent Garden.

The American premiere of *The Knot Garden* took place at the Cahn Auditorium, Northwestern, on 22 February 1974 and was in fact the first stage production of any of Tippett's operas in America. Bernard Rubenstein conducted. The student cast was an admirable one; and the opera made a great impact on its audiences at both of its two performances.

As soon as the second of these performances was over, Tippett went on a trip to New Mexico with Don Roberts and his wife. They flew to El Paso and drove via Juarez, Albuquerque, and the Chaco Canyon to the Hopi reservation, where they stayed at the Tribal Motel. On the Saturday night at Hotevilla there were sacred ceremonies in the kivas (underground ceremonial chambers). Don Roberts described these in a letter saying:

Hotevilla is perhaps the most traditional of all the Hopi villages. The three of us went into the kiva and watched the kachina dances. These are dances done by masked beings who are representing various spirits. The kachinas

*From an interview with *Lively Arts* editor, Dorothy Andries, Evanston, 14 February 1974.

are extremely sacred and when the human being puts the mask on, he is considered to be that particular kachina and can make only the sounds and motions of that spirit. Hotevilla does not allow electricity in the village, so all you have for light are a couple of Coleman gas lanterns hanging from the ceiling. The kivas are small, maybe five yards by twenty yards, and the dance group may range from twelve to forty people. Sometimes they're accompanied by drums; but usually at Hotevilla you have only the singers accompanying themselves with rattles and shells tied on their legs. The whole sound, the setting, and the experience are from another world.

The following day the party drove to Phoenix and flew back to Chicago, where Tippett conducted three performances of his Symphony no. 3 and Piano Concerto with the Chicago Symphony Orchestra. This led to a commission from that orchestra for a new symphony (no. 4) to be delivered by 1977.

Back in England, he resumed the composition of his fourth opera, *The Ice Break*, where he had left off before flying to America, near the end of Act I. Act II was finished by February 1975, and Act III a year later. Advantage was taken of the opera's premiere in London (Covent Garden, 7 July 1977) to organize an exhibition of photographs, manuscripts, designs, programmes, press cuttings and other related material under the title 'A Man of Our Time' at the Covent Garden Gallery, 20 Russell Street, during the month of July; and an illustrated catalogue was issued. Symphony no. 4 followed the opera without a break and was ready on time for its Chicago premiere under Sir George Solti in October 1977.

Having completed his fourth opera and fourth symphony, he now decided to write a fourth string quartet, his first for over thirty years; but he interrupted this composition in order to visit the United States in January 1978 for a conducting engagement in Dallas. There he fell ill. At the last moment David Atherton was engaged as his substitute, and Tippett returned to England. Back at home, he made a remarkably swift recovery and by February was well enough to set off for Australia via Bali, where, like so many visiting musicians, he was entranced by the gamelan music. In Australia he attended the Perth and Adelaide festivals. The programme of the Perth Festival featured much of his chamber music, and also a performance of *A Child of Our Time*. At the Adelaide Festival he attended the premiere of the first production of *The Midsummer Marriage* outside Europe, and this proved to be a great popular success. He also conducted the second performance of his fourth symphony. He gave a lecture in the Sydney Opera House before flying home across the Pacific, stopping in California to conduct a performance of *A Child of Our Time* in Los Angeles. Back in England, he barely had time to resume the interrupted composition of his fourth string quartet before he was invited to Kiel for the first German production of *The Ice Break* (26 June 1978). The quartet was finished in September; and this left him free to tackle a work he had long wanted to undertake, namely, a Triple Concerto for Violin, Viola, Cello and Orchestra.

In 1979 *Music of the Angels*, a new selection of his broadcast talks, essays, reviews and miscellaneous papers, was published under the editorship of Meirion Bowen. Of particular interest in this collection were 'The Nameless Hero' (four talks on *A Child of Our Time*); the Sketch for a Modern Oratorio (i.e. *A Child of Our Time*) which Tippett drafted in 1938 at the request of T. S. Eliot; early sketch-book material showing the genesis of *The Midsummer Marriage*; a batch of essays and commentaries on *King Priam*; and a revised version of a set of unscripted talks, *Love in Opera*, originally broadcast by the Canadian Broadcasting Corporation.

For an artist who has shown no special deference towards the Establishment, Tippett has been offered, and has accepted, a large number and wide variety of honours and awards. In January 1949 he received the Cobbett Medal for Chamber Music. He was created a Commander of the British Empire in 1959 and knighted in 1966. A spate of honorary doctorates started about the same time – Cambridge (1964); Trinity College, Dublin (1964); Leeds (1965); York (1966); Oxford (1967); Leicester (1968); University of Wales (1968); Bristol (1970); Bath (1972); Warwick (1974); University of London (1975); Sheffield (1976); Birmingham (1976); Lancaster (1977). He was elected a Fellow of the Royal College of Music in 1961, and an honorary member of the American Academy of Arts and Letters in 1973. In 1976 he gave the Doty Lectures in Fine Art at the University of Austin, Texas. He was elected an extraordinary member of the Akademie der Künste, Berlin, in 1976; and the same year he was awarded the Gold Medal of the Royal Philharmonic Society. In 1978 he was elected a foreign honorary member of the American Academy of Arts and Sciences, and also became a corresponding member of the Bavarian Academy of Fine Arts. Of all the words of glowing praise contained in the citations to these awards few are likely to have given him greater pleasure than those of the Cambridge Orator (20 February 1964):

There follows another interpreter of Apollo,* who can truly be called 'A Child of Our Time', the title of an admirable work he produced amid the fury of the Second World War, which first made his name widely known. With his friend on whom we have conferred a like degree, Benjamin Britten, he has much in common: there is the same subtle sense of appropriateness when they set words to music, the same horror of war, the same pity for the sufferings of the human race. 'Look at *Priam*' (to quote Aeneas):
sunt lacrimae rerum et mentem mortalia tangunt.
The opera he composed, both words and music, under the name of that King is a tragedy; but his other opera, *The Midsummer Marriage*, should be called a comedy, if we class as a comedy that famous work not dissimilar in genus, *The Magic Flute*. But the truth is that whatever this man touches he philosophizes. Whence he has often been invited to broadcast his opinions on the radio, and has written much for journals and collections, sometimes indeed in the oracular manner of Heraclitus, but always acute, penetrating and provocative of thought. He has also shown himself an excellent teacher as Director of Music for eleven years at Morley College, inspiring his pupils with love for himself and for his art of music. But first and foremost he is a producer of delectable sounds, using in this the same intelligence and the same professional rigour, whether as an interpreter conducting choir and orchestra he is eliciting harmonious execution, or whether as a creator breathing 'air from another planet' he is meditating new and divine compositions.

But what of the man behind the façade of these numerous honours and awards?

The first thing to say is that he has been unspoilt by all this praise and fame. For the last half century he has lived a quiet dedicated life in the country – in Oxted, Wadhurst and Wiltshire – where he has written virtually all his compositions. At various times he has travelled widely. In his boyhood and youth he got to know many parts of the British Isles. Probably the West Country holds his special allegiance, maybe because of his Cornish descent and its special link with the Celtic world. Other allegiances go even further back, almost to the dawn of history; and prehistoric remains like Avebury and Silbury in Wiltshire hold a deep chthonic resonance for him.

Both the festivals he has been associated with – St Ives and Bath – were situated in the West Country. St Ives lasted only one year; but I have reason to remember how exhilarated he was by the atmosphere.

*Here the Orator is referring to the fact that at this investiture Tippett followed immediately after Sir Arthur Bliss, then Master of the Queen's Music.

At the end of an evening concert of part songs and choruses held on the terrace of the Tregenna Castle Hotel with its fabulous view of the north coast of Cornwall, he suddenly seized me by the arm and with a whoop of abandon rushed me off headlong down the precipitous slope that leads towards the harbour. This was the result of a spontaneous outburst of *joie de vivre*, characteristic of his natural gaiety.

Tippett is a great conversationalist. The two books of his collected papers – *Moving into Aquarius* and *Music of the Angels* – give an idea of the wide range of his interests, touching on political, social, psychological, philosophical and esthetic matters. The script of 'Poets in a Barren Age', printed in the revised edition of *Moving into Aquarius*, is particularly revealing of the way in which he regards himself and his vocation. In it he recalled the fact that he had been writing music for forty years or more, a period during which there had been world-shattering events, but he had gone on writing because he knew he must and because his true function within society was to continue an age-old tradition:

This tradition is to create images from the depths of the imagination and to give them form whether visual, intellectual or musical. For it is only through images that the inner world communicates at all. Images of the past, shapes of the future. Images of vigour for a decadent period, images of calm for one too violent. Images of reconciliation for worlds torn by division. And in an age of mediocrity and shattered dreams, images of abounding, generous, exuberant beauty.

But fascinating though his broadcasts and lectures are to reread, it must be admitted that they lose a dimension on the printed page without the lively sound of his voice broadcasting to millions or speaking to an intimate gathering of friends. And that is natural and understandable, for sound is his medium, and above all the sound of music. A highly developed auditory imagination is part of his inner life. Working in the mornings in his music-room, he stands at a draughtsman's board, and the interior procession of sounds moving slowly through his mind is exposed in cross section and fixed in notation – in the case of an orchestral work, direct into full score. Once I asked him whether the actual sound of his music was always the same as the ideal sound in his imagination. 'Usually,' he replied, 'though once or twice I've been unable to find the right notation for it at the first go.'

At the head of this chapter I have placed a saying of Parolles from

All's Well That Ends Well that Tippett chose as epigraph for *The Knot Garden* – '*simply the thing I am shall make me live.*' It seems to me that in its widest and deepest senses this is characteristic of the lifelong dedication of the composer to his muse. Doubtless much more has been sacrificed than we may realise. Nevertheless, it is probably true to say, '*simply the thing he is has made him live.*'

2

An Oratorio before the Operas
A Child of Our Time

In 1938 Tippett felt the need to embark on a large-scale work for voices and orchestra. The previous year he had finished a piece for chorus and orchestra entitled *A Song of Liberty*, to a text from William Blake's *The Marriage of Heaven and Hell*; but he was dissatisfied with it and after a single performance never allowed it to be published or performed. Instead, his thoughts turned to the possibility of writing an opera or an oratorio, and he began to cast about for a suitable subject. At first he had it in mind to write an opera based on the Irish rebellion of Easter 1916, but eventually he dropped this idea because (as he put it) 'the dramatic impulse was receding before the contemplative', and this for him was decisive. He now saw that the new work would belong to the concert hall (or church) and not the opera house, and that it would be written in the tradition of the Passions, where the story is related only as the basis for contemplation.

Shortly after the period of Munich, as has been mentioned, a young Polish Jewish refugee called Herschel Grynsban, driven to desperation by the persecution of his family, shot the German diplomat von Rath in Paris, an act that led almost immediately to a savage retaliatory pogrom in central Europe. Grynsban's trial in January 1939 drew international attention to the case. Here possibly was the raw material for the work Tippett had in mind. The characters of the action, if such it may be called, would be the Boy himself; his Mother, Uncle, Aunt; a Narrator to bind the argument together; and a chorus which could appear as the Oppressed, the Self-Righteous, and a double chorus of Persecutors and Persecuted.

As Tippett contemplated the form his new work was to take, he recalled that there were two musical traditions of arrangement that had always fascinated him: the scheme of Handel's *Messiah*, and the scheme of the Lutheran Passions:

The shape of *Messiah* is tripartite. The first part is all prophecy and prep-aration. The second part is epic: from the birth of Christ to the second coming, judgement, millenium, and world's end. The third part is meditative: chiefly the words of St Paul. . . . I decided to accept this format for *A Child of Our Time* by keeping a first part entirely general, restricting the epic material to a second part, and using a third part for consequential comment.*

He then pointed out that the scheme of the Lutheran *Passions* was more unitary, based as it must be on the liturgical gospel except for Passion Sunday; but that within it the traditional musico-verbal functions could always be distinguished – narrational recitative, des-criptive chorus, contemplative aria, and finally the special Protestant constituent of the congregational hymn. He wanted to use *all* these functional practices within the tripartite shape borrowed from *Messiah*.

An immediate difficulty arose over the 'congregational hymn'. In a world trembling on the brink of a second World War, where stan-dards of morality were crumbling, and Christianity could speak for no more than a fraction of the world population, what 'hymns' could command the consensus of the sort of congregation that would gather in concert halls to listen to *A Child of Our Times*? The composer has described this dilemma.

For some time I was at a loss. Then one never-to-be-forgotten Sunday, I heard a coloured singer on the radio sing Negro songs, including the spiritual 'Steal away'. At the phrase 'The trumpet sounds within-a my soul', I was blessed with an immediate intuition: that I was being moved by this phrase in some way beyond what the musical phrase in itself warranted. I realised that in England or America everyone would be moved in this way, forcing me to see that the unique verbal and musical metaphor for this particular function in this particular oratorio had been found. But it was not until after the world war, which soon supervened, that I could test in performance the fact that the Negro spiritual presented no expressional barriers anywhere in Europe. Nor maybe anywhere in the world.†

After sending to America for a collection of spirituals, he chose five for their tunes and their words, which fitted five calculated situations

*From Michael Tippett, 'T. S. Eliot and *A Child of Our Time*', in *Music of the Angels* (edited by Meirion Bowen, Eulenburg, 1979).
†*Ibid.*

in the scheme of his new work. These he used, not as congregational hymns in the sense that Britten was later to weave two great hymns (to be sung by the whole congregation) into the musical texture of *Noyes Fludde*, but as integral parts of the oratorio and to be performed as such. The plan of the new work was now virtually complete; and there remained only the question of the libretto.

During the past few years Tippett had got to know T. S. Eliot quite well. His early verse play, *Murder in the Cathedral*, had achieved a great popular success after its initial production at the Canterbury Festival of 1935; but Tippett had found his subsequent verse play, *The Family Reunion*, even more powerful and significant. He now asked Eliot if he would consent to write the text for his oratorio. This Eliot agreed to do, provided he was given a scheme of musical numbers and an exact account of the number and kinds of words considered necessary for each musical section. Tippett returned home and drafted what he called a 'Sketch for a Modern Oratorio'.* He had already done so much advance work on this idea that he was able to set down straightaway a musical-dramatic scheme which in the event remained virtually unchanged. Eliot considered this 'Sketch' for some weeks and then gave Tippett the somewhat surprising advice that he should write the words himself. He felt the 'Sketch' was already a text in embryo and that whatever words he or any other poet might write would be of such greater *poetic* quality that they would 'stick out a mile'. Some years later he wrote to me,† explaining that

the words for an oratorio should be either very familiar to an audience (a condition which Biblical oratorios satisfy) or if they cannot be familiar, they should be very simple. It seemed to me that there was no point in getting me or any other poet to provide words for that purpose.

Tippett accepted Eliot's judgement and wrote the libretto of *A Child Of Our Time* himself.

On the whole the drafting of it went smoothly and effectively. The composer found he could use much of the material he had already sketched out for Eliot with little or no change. It is true there were occasional infelicities of expression. For instance, the text of the tenor solo in Part I runs as follows:

I have no money for my bread; I have no gift for my love.
I am caught between my desires and their frustration as between the

*Reprinted in *Music of the Angels*.
†In a letter dated 29 March 1955.

    hammer and the anvil.
   How can I grow to a man's stature?

Here the first and last sentences are admirably idiomatic and direct, whereas the second sentence is an awkward piece of periphrastic metaphor which gets mercifully consumed in the musical development of the song and so is hardly noticed by the audience. For the brief text needed for the 'Chorus of the Oppressed' Tippett eventually varied a sentence from Isaiah to read

   When shall the usurer's city cease?

and this tongue-twister with its nest of sibilants turned out to be an onomatopoeic triumph when sung as a fugue by a four-part choir at an *allegro non troppo* speed.

   But Tippett was particularly successful with the words for the impressive choruses that preface each of the three parts, and which, in the composer's parlance, formed a kind of 'Prologue in Heaven' on the analogy of Goethe's *Faust*. The conflated texts of these three prologue-choruses read as follows:

PART I   The world turns on its dark side.
               It is winter.
PART I   A star rises in midwinter.
               Behold the man! The scapegoat!
PART III The cold deepens.
               The world descends into the icy waters
               where lies the jewel of great price.

A similar style of utterance is to be found in the General Ensemble at the end of Part III:

   I would know my shadow and my light,
   So shall I at last be whole.
   Then, courage, brother, dare the grave passage.
   Here is no final grieving, but an abiding hope.
   The moving waters renew the earth.
   It is spring.

The deliberate emphasis on darkness and light is echoed by the choice of the following half-line from *Murder in the Cathedral* as epigraph: ' . . . the darkness declares the glory of light'. But it is worth remembering that in a note accompanying the 1975 recording of this work, the composer's comment on the Boy's final affirmation, 'I would know my shadow and my light, so shall I at last be whole', was that this was 'a sentence very easy to say, very difficult to do'. He thought it might be just possible for individuals, 'but impossible for collectives in our present climate of self-righteousness; of groups, societies, nations'.

The choice of the negro spirituals had an important effect on the musical vocabulary of the oratorio. The composer found that 'harmonization' in the conventional sense was not called for. Instead, he accepted the underlying conventional chord of the added seventh particular to each spiritual, and often sought variety only through rhythmic counterpoint, and by playing tonal masses of choral sound off against solo-voiced leaders. The consequently harmonically static choruses at the five critical points provided a peculiar contrast to the much more harmonically ambiguous music of the other members. They became periods of rest.*

As for the general style in which the sophisticated numbers of the oratorio were written, the composer

used the interval of a minor third produced so characteristically in the melodies of the spirituals when moving from the fifth of the tonic to the flat seventh, as a basic interval of the whole work – sometimes on its own, sometimes superimposed upon the open fifth below the lower note.†

The idiom of these sophisticated numbers sometimes recalls that of German contemporary anti-Nazi composers such as Paul Hindemith and Kurt Weill.

After the first performance of *A Child of Our Time*, a number of critics and some members of the public felt that the wilful admixture of popular and sophisticated music caused a kind of dichotomy in the score; but in the course of time it became accepted that the spirituals had their own part to play in the musical scheme of the oratorio, and the 'transitions to them are regarded as effective'.‡ These bridge passages, where the composer gives advance warning of the arrival of a spiritual have a particularly moving quality about them. They represent a change of musical gear that releases strong feelings of compassion. As the composer has said, '*A Child of Our Time* makes its effect in fact more by the unity and intensity of the mood than by its formal shape.'

After such a prolonged and carefully considered gestation, it is hardly surprising that when at last Tippett started to compose *A Child*

*From 'T. S. Eliot and *A Child of Our Time*'.
†*Ibid.*
‡*Ibid.*

of Our Time, the music came with a rush. The first bars were written in September 1939 a few days after the outbreak of war, and the score was finished by 1941. The musical idiom employed was deliberately a simple one, and the style of instrumentation unsophisticated. Only medium forces were called for. Nevertheless, in wartime conditions there was no likelihood of an early performance being given: so the composer put the score aside to await a more propitious moment. This came earlier than might have been thought possible. A number of musical well-wishers, including Walter Goehr, Benjamin Britten and Peter Pears, were anxious that it should be put on; and their interest led to an enthusiastic, but somewhat 'scratch' matinee performance at the Adelphi Theatre, London, on 19 March 1944. When the war ended, it was found that the work appealed with equal directness to audiences at home and abroad; and since then it has always retained its popularity.

3
Quest and Celebration
The Midsummer Marriage

Once *A Child of Our Time* had been launched and the war was seen to be drawing to a conclusion, Tippett felt the need to compose two major works – a symphony and an opera. The Symphony (1944–5), called Symphony no. 1 to distinguish it from the Symphony in B flat (1933–4), an early, rejected and unpublished work, was first performed by the Liverpool Philharmonic Orchestra conducted by Malcolm Sargent at the Philharmonic Hall, Liverpool, in November 1945. Work on the opera started about 1946.

Whereas before the war it had been difficult if, not impossible, for an English opera composer to know where to place a new opera of his, post-war conditions were beginning to show signs of improvement. Indeed, a boost had been given to English opera generally by the success of Benjamin Britten's *Peter Grimes* when launched at Sadler's Wells Theatre in June 1945, and by the re-opening of the Royal Opera House, Covent Garden, in 1946 with the promise that in the future permanent opera and ballet companies would be based on that theatre.

The genesis of *The Midsummer Marriage* is well attested. About the time of its premiere the composer wrote five articles for *The Observer* on 'The Birth of an Opera', which were later reprinted in *Moving into Aquarius*. There he made it clear that he realized that the use of the word 'marriage' in his title must imply a comedy, 'for [he wrote] there is only one comic plot: the unexpected hindrances to an eventual marriage'. As leading man and woman he took a couple whose illusions were spiritual – George (as the hero was originally called) and Jennifer – and matched them against a second man and second woman (soubrette) whose illusions were social. 'So [he wrote] the eventual marriage of the first pair became a spiritual, even super-

natural, symbol, transcending the purely social and biological signifi-
cance of the eventual marriage of the second pair' – Jack and Bella.
The two pairs were interconnected in so far as Jennifer's father, King
Fisher, employed Bella as his secretary and (later on) Jack as his motor
mechanic.

It was at this point that Tippett experienced what he called his
'first illumination':

that is I *saw* a stage picture (as opposed to hearing a musical sound) of a
wooded hilltop with a temple, where a warm and soft young man was being
rebuffed by a cold and hard young woman (to my mind a very common
present situation) to such a degree that the collective, magical archetypes
take charge – Jung's *anima* and *animus* – the girl, inflated by the latter, rises
through the stage flies to heaven, and the man, overwhelmed by the former,
descends through the stage floor to hell. But it was clear they would soon
return. For I saw the girl later descending in a costume reminiscent of the
goddess Athena (who was born without father from Zeus's head) and the
man ascending in one reminiscent of the god Dionysus (who, son of earth-
born Semele, had a second birth from Zeus's thigh).

Even as I write now some of the excitement of these first pictures comes
back. It is the feeling a creative artist has when he knows he has become
the instrument of some collective imaginative experience. . . .*

The musical implications of this vision were important. They called
not only for contrasting musical movements for the young woman's
ascent to heaven and the young man's descent to hell, but also for a
reversal of values when in their turn the young man ascended to
heaven and the young woman descended to hell. Even then the movement was not complete, for the young couple had still to return to
their base after their trials and transformations. This postulated a
lengthy musical exposition in Act I, which in its turn postulated large-
scale musical developments and summaries in the following acts. It
was as if the composer, after intending to write a concerto, had discovered that what he really wanted to create was a *double* concerto.

From the beginning Tippett felt free to make use of the findings
of anthropology, mythology and deep psychology to help him express
his themes. The setting was chosen as a place where the natural and
the supernatural could 'naturally' meet and interact, rather in the
spirit of Shakespeare's *A Midsummer Night's Dream*. The manners

*From 'The Birth of an Opera' in *Moving into Aquarius* (Routledge & Kegan Paul,
1959; Paladin, 1974).

and costumes of the 'natural' world were to be of the present; and the manifestations of the supernatural world (e.g. the Ancients and the young dancer Strephon) were to be related to ancient Greek modes. With the aid of this apparatus he reckoned he could assimilate the visionary as well as the realistic and satirical elements in his action, just as Mozart had succeeded in doing more or less the same thing in *The Magic Flute*.

Once again an important decision had to be taken about the libretto. In the letter from T. S. Eliot about oratorio librettos quoted above the poet dramatist went on to say:

Opera is a different matter, and while I don't think that a really poetic gift is necessary, I do feel that the author of an operatic libretto should have some theatrical gift.

But after the success of *A Child of Our Time*, there was no doubt in Tippett's mind. He would write the libretto himself. Even if he had wanted to engage an outside librettist, it would have been extremely difficult for him to give precise advance instructions about what he wanted, for he was beginning to find that frequently his stage action was dictated by the musical ideas he had germinating in his mind rather than the reverse. This meant that when sometime in 1946 he came to tackle Act I, he found himself working on words and music (full score) more or less simultaneously – an unusual, not to say irregular, state of affairs, since normal operatic procedure is for the libretto to be completed before the score is composed.

A faithful, blow-by-blow account of the way Tippett worked at the words and music of *The Midsummer Marriage* emerges from a series of letters he wrote me during the years 1948–55. These were not carefully drafted epistles, but rough notes struck off in the heat of the moment – conversational in tone, at times almost telegraphically terse – and they offer a fascinating glimpse of the opera composer in the act of creation. It is true that they give only one side of a dialogue into which I entered with great relish, but it seemed to me there was no need to print any of my own part in this correspondence, since either what I had to say could be easily deduced from the composer's comments and answers; or if there was something in his letters needing elucidation, that could best be covered by a few explanatory notes. The letters are not always dated, but where dates are missing, I've usually been able to supply an approximate date based on internal evidence, or a postmark. Apart from a few cuts, the text has not been edited. Even contractions and abbreviations are preserved.

The first letter of the series is the only one that does not mention the opera. It refers to a performance of Tippett's Symphony no. 1 I had just heard.

Whitegate Cottage   [February 1948]
    Oxted
      Sy

Wed.

Dear Eric,

What you said on Monday gave me great encouragement. For, though – while being well aware of my deficiencies – I have a deep, underlying confidence in the *temper* of the work. I am not so inhuman that I don't have misgivings when the external, material success is slower than it might be. The Symphony is being taken up by the Third Programme, for example, but not into any commercial series of metropolitan or provincial concerts. So that I *can* easily begin to feel that the deficiencies are overwhelming, and that the piece is rightly discarded, before it has been heard! Just because it savours of too much conceit to be quite sure it *will* be worth a more common place in the repertoire eventually. It is encouraging to have an unexpected assent of some sort from those more sensitive musicians, who cannot be accused of personal bias, as I must accuse myself, or those very close to me.

Anyhow – it is down for a studio performance on Thurs March 25 – Third Prog. – Goehr & Symphony Orch. Can you apply for tickets yourself? Or shall I do it for you?

The enclosed leaflets show a concert which clashes I'm afraid, by great bad luck, with 3rd Symphony, Stravinsky. So I expect you must go there. We do repeat 'Child' for the Cambridge Theatre people on the Sun. aft. March 7th, the Sun. following in fact. (We do a shortened version for Mayer's Children's Concert on the day between).

Please give the leaflets away or post or drop in the street. Love to you both, and all –

Michael

The book mentioned in the following letter is *The Rise of English Opera*, which I had contracted to write for John Lehmann's new publishing house. Dodo was the name of my wife.

Whitegate Cottage   [September 1948]
    Oxted
    Sy

Dear Eric,

No! the 'Midsummer Marriage' will *not* be completed or performed by Christmas 1949. The position is the following . . . by New Year the first Act will be finished in score, text, and a pf. reduction made by an ex-student of mine. You can have this at your convenience and for the length of time you might want. As this Act is pretty representative of the sort of thing I'm up to, it won't be too bad. If you then want it, I could let you see the draft of the rest of the text. It's only a sketch – because, while the scenes (in continental sense) won't probably get altered now in substance, I'm learning all the time to write text and music almost together, scene by scene. Finally – we might meet and have a short talk about it, if any help. There's too a script of a BBC Talk wh. says something of what I've been dreaming of. I'm very glad you want to mention it in the book, because it might help a lot towards comprehension of this admittedly risky opera. Risky in that it flies higher than I expect I have capacity to accomplish. But whose Icarian collapse may well help someone better to fly safely. And *please* – if you do see the finished Act, you must speak candidly that I may be helped to improvements. I'm so engulfed by it, that I can't always see the trees for the wood. But they may as well be nice ones in the end, by attention to their single shapes.

I wanted to be going where you are at that time, but must go to Budapest on the Bartok Jury – for my sins.

                                                    Yours
                                                    Michael

Tutte le parole graziose a Dodo.

The 'book on Ben' in the next letter was the first edition of my monograph on Benjamin Britten and his operas, which was originally published by Atlantis Verlag, Zurich, and Boosey & Hawkes, London, in 1948, revised and reprinted in 1953, and republished in a much expanded form by Faber & Faber in association with Boosey & Hawkes in 1970.

Michael Tippett in the Wiltshire countryside, 1975 (*Scorer*)

Tippett, Sam Wanamaker (left) and Ralph Koltai during a rehearsal of the Welsh National Opera (*Southern*)

Tippett, Ralph Koltai and Richard Armstrong during a rehearsal of the Welsh National Opera, 1977 (*Sheppard*)

Tippett at a recording session with Colin Davis (*Evans*)

The composer at work on the Ms of his Third Symphony (*Thomson Newspapers Ltd*)

Tippett and Benjamin Britten at a party to celebrate Tippett's sixtieth birthday (*Auerbach*)

Michael Tippett Mus. Doc. in procession with Sir Arthur Bliss, Master of the Queen's Music, Cambridge, 20 February 1964 (*Cambridge News*)

THE MIDSUMMER MARRIAGE: first page of the ink full score. (The remaining pages of this score have disappeared.)

THE MIDSUMMER MARRIAGE: first production at Covent Garden (1955), with scenery and costumes by Barbara Hepworth. *Above:* Joan Sutherland as Jenifer and Richard Lewis as Mark (*Rogers*). *Below:* Adele Leigh as Bella and Otakar Kraus as King Fisher (*Rogers*)

THE MIDSUMMER MARRIAGE: The second production at Covent Garden (1968), designed by Tony Walton. *Above:* The appearance of Madam Sosostris in Act III (*Rogers*). *Below:* One of the Ritual Dances (*Crickmay*)

Whitegates Cottage   [December 1948]
   Oxted
     Sy

My dear Eric,

Thanks so much for your letter and the book on Ben. I haven't yet read the latter thoroughly, but it seems to me at a glance excellent for its purpose. I saw 'Grimes' recently in Budapest: a very good performance – less sentimental, and dramatically tauter than Sadlers Wells. I never saw Covent Garden. Two visits abroad (now I feel to have been mistakes) and the music for the royal babe, and a consequent week's illness due to over-work has held the opera up. But I'm now on the last lap of the first act, and if you can hang on for a bit I'd prefer to let you have the whole Act at one go.

I have to be in London on Jan 11th to receive the Cobbett Medal for Chamber Music – which function is at 6 – p'raps we cld lunch that day? then I wld be better able to estimate the closing date of composition on Act 1. Let me have a card sometime to know if it's alright – & when & where.

Yrs
Michael.

Oxted   [June 1949]

Dear Eric,

Herewith script and provisional preface – which I'm inclined to think shld not be used.

The early scenes, or parts of them, are too colloquial for my 2-years-later taste – & I'm going to do one or two pieces again. It's also the old problem of getting argumentation over & out of the way, musically. The later parts succeed better. In fact the 2nd half of the act, the last 2 scenes in fact, which play about 25' out of the 55', have come out rather well, I think, without hitches & dramatic. The great 'ensemble of perplexity' before the finale is quite nicely placed for the whole Act, & I'm bucked with the overall shape.

See you later.

Michael.

On 3 August 1949 there was an informal run-through of Act I of *The Midsummer Marriage* in my flat at Cholmley Gardens, West Hampstead, while my wife was away on holiday. These flats, which are built round a garden area featuring lawns, tennis courts and garages, were being repainted that afternoon; and I remember that the Irish decorators, who must have been rather surprised at the sounds emanating from no. 55, occasionally retaliated with fragments of *The Last Rose of Summer*. Those present at this run-through included the composer, Hans Schmidt-Isserstedt, John Minchinton, Michael Tillett (who had arranged the vocal score), and myself.

Oxted   [10 August 1949]
Wed.

My dear Eric,

Your letter came in this morning & many thanks for it. I had had as you know some misgivings that do come up from time to time always in any serious artist's life – that is to say, I generalise with perhaps too much complacence – but I suspect all the same it is so. I had a special fear about the effect of the whole proceeding, on Isserstedt – whom I had not myself invited, but whom Hartog had – thinking it to be advantageous. And Isserstedt is one of the channels thro which news of the opera reaches Rennert, the very go-ahead producer at the Hamburg Opera. Luckily Isserstedt is good enough a chap not to make judgments where they can't in fairness be categorically made – & in any case he appears to have been certain that there were lovely things in the opera. And even proposes (still thro Hartog – his closest English friend) that he comes here later in the autumn & discusses some scoring points with consideration & at leisure. So that will be naturally accepted with pleasure – for, so long as I don't get myself into a knot between varying expert opinions, I believe in colleagues' guidance & advice wherever possible.

Therefore your letter encourages me further – and you'll be glad to know that I've been at work making the script for Act 2. I shall send you the draft later – for curiosity. I find that this time – after the 2½ years lessons of Act I, I am better at the game. That is – I can go further to resolve the whole theatrical situation in terms of music & invent a pattern of words already related ahead to the dramatico-musical needs. The process is now closer. Less that of being fascinated by the too externally contrived words, which one then uses every art to dissolve into the music.

This question of repeats you mention. I hadn't been aware that I had repeated so much. But maybe we're thinking of the same place, i.e. the big scene for King Fisher alone (Sc 6 I think it is) where he gets the chorus off the stage – first the men and then the girls. He has a strophic aria – & I have had already trouble, thro a slight shift in the story, to re-set his second verse in terms of differently persuading the girls & their refusal of his money. But I have at the back of my mind before, & now much more fully since playing through the Act, had the feeling that the *music* has altered the original conception. That is – that I have written such a tremendous Strophe for him, it won't do to repeat it entire, however subtly changed. It needs at all events compression – if not a whole new music suited much more clearly to the dramatic necessities of his sentimental appeal to the girls – if the patter-presto coda can yet be saved. What I would be glad of from you – is your comment eventually on this instance of my own, &, with regard to instances that you see which I'm not so aware of, whether (at a much later stage for me, not now, when I want to do Act 2 at a go) there are places in your opinion where the repeated material already is ineffective for the reasons you mention – & *should* be overhauled. Perhaps it might be enough to say now simply 'yes' or 'no', but not to tell me exactly what till Act 2 at least is also in the stage to be looked at by you with a fresh & critical eye. For what is sure is that I *have* had a tremendous sense of relief and release by finishing the huge Act I, and that to return to it at present is both impossible & fatal. Goehr had already given me v. good advice on that. For it's also certain that each act slightly alters the relative importance of what's gone before etc. etc.

Incidentally – & to return – I have remembered a scene where the repeat of material did already disturb me – that of the Voice warning from behind the Gates etc. – that is to say I had been conscious of it even *musically*. Well – it had better wait till final revisions are undertaken. And all I ask from you now is that you could note as circumstantially as you can afford energy & time what strikes you & note in so permanent a manner that we could together take the matter up at some suitable & profitable moment.

Your comment about Jack's quatrain is fascinating. Michael Tillett had already come across one or two such – & it's sure that only someone other than I can notice them, because I am doomed to my own initial parti pris. Of the final chord – Tillett had already complained – & I had also been unsure. For musically it's a matter between 2 & 3-bar-rhythm – as you can see by a fresh test. The initial B flat motif ('We are the laughing children') is in 2-bar rhythm. But the consequent music ('Rough, raw, rude' or whatever it is) is in 3-bar rhythm. The last held chord is in 2 again, as I have been thinking. Tillett thinks it in 3. But I am less sure that it wasn't a 4 bar. Perhaps your solution is the real answer – because I had realised I needed to ask someone about the curtain & what is best. So later – I'll probably try out what you suggest.

And now – so much does the work engage me that I'd forgotten I'd meant to write and answer the other questions. (And still I have some of my own!) . . .

Act 2 script is working out quite fun. Has, outside the first Ritual dances, much less flighty goings-on & is nearer to wholesome opera buffa. I'm hoping to let it be certainly more tender (Jack & Bella) & occasionally more humorous – even slightly satirical. It scarcely advances the 'story' at all – but serves rather to separate the tremendous Acts & to give the real characters – Jack & Bella – who never see the visionary moments – & who have an intense life of their own dissociated from the accidents of their being involved with the others – a chance to present themselves a bit clearer. Also – in the initial dances – as you will see – for the only occasion we (the audience) see the 'Other world' at play with no real stage character around. A different dimension & which is I'm afraid probably too sharply run slap up against Jack's & Bella's domestic troubles. But may be that's how the world is. The transitions – whether gradual or by jerk & contrast – are really fascinating to operate. I use quite a different sense for them. With a pretty intense stage picture which I always have before me, I 'feel around' so to speak for the 'pressures' of the various worlds of apprehension coming up within the characters present. This is I think what I am learning better. One has of course to start somehow. But the beginning of the script, at any rate, shows a too detached verbal play. I mean – the verbal meanings tend to detach themselves as a thing in itself. But of course in any opera, or stage piece, you have to get quite a lot at the start cleared out of the way somehow. Hence the various clever devices such as the prologuial scenes e.g. 'Grimes'. I'm always searching for stage movements wh however slight can 'do' the meanings for us e.g. Ancients tripping Strephon etc. Act I was always the worst & the most complicated. The others 'run' more easily, as you'll see in time! My wishes to Dodo & Sarah, the unknown.

Michael

As a result of the run-through of Act I of *The Midsummer Marriage* I had written to the composer with a number of queries. One was whether he was correct in his use of the (Italian) direction *Tempo d'avanti*. Another: should George know Strephon's name when the dancer is tripped up by the Ancients? The script of Act II enclosed with this letter was that of an early draft, in which the action started with the four ritual dances (there called 'racing dances') and continued with a longish scene for Jack and Bella, who were joined by King Fisher and a Messenger, who tried to attract attention by blowing a whistle. Later the Messenger was dropped.

Oxted   [28 August 1949]

Dear Eric,

Thanks a lot for the letter. I read it in bed for I had one of my stomach upsets (the first since the last year's crisis) as the result of leaving the composition to go one day to see to the regularisation of a run-away marriage at Wolverhampton. I hardly dare leave the house! But today I hope to get back to my own 'Marriage'.

I expect you're right about avanti – in fact you must be. But 'primo' may not do. Anyhow that can be made clear by some means.

George knowing Strephon's name? In my mind I had always supposed G. must have known the Ancients (as he later says) 'since boyhood'. That this relationship is one of the few facts (!) in the story. So that presumably he knew Strephon's name. But Tillett had already been worried by the same thing. And he had suggested that to avoid trouble it were just best not to name him at all. Or at least for G. not to call him by name. It's another matter we can decide on bit by bit. (This process of getting things right by common consent was widely followed, & successfully, in 'Child of Our Time'. I value it v. much).

I like the idea of photographing 2 pages of the score & I'm sure Schotts will amplify my consent. I'll ring Steffens tomorrow & let you know confirmation of my surmise by phone or card. You know – I have quite a lot of hopes of much good (to me & the opera) coming from your book. Because it is by gradual & slow dissemination & assimilation that the producers & public will be formed. At some time or other I think it will almost appear natural & inevitable that the opera is to be 'given to the world'. And it may well turn out that this moment won't be too distant from the date of completion.

I'm enclosing (for your amusement if not critical comment) the draft script of Act 2. The dances of Scene I will need a bit better & different description. I'm at them now – & the music. I've had a useful talk with a stage dancer. I reckon the Prelude & Dances will take 8-9 minutes. Rather longer than I had originally expected (the whole Act will be abt. 25'). It's the only occasion where the Supernaturals appear by themselves (like Puck & the Fairies) & the scene will have a curious effect by its v. absence of voices. The dances are ritualistic leading if permitted to the death and dismemberment of the [Sear?] King in the

Service of the White Goddess. I hope to get the atmosphere to hover between play & 'drama' – with the uncanny not too dominant a note, but in the background. It makes I'm afraid a most sharp contrast to the Jack-Bella domesticities. And the Messenger! He was originally conceived as rather more sentimental – small with a piping voice & he accepted the shilling. Now I see him as tougher & as even 'further on' in the generation sequence than Jack & Bella & the others. Hence I came at 'No tipping in our service' – but 'service' isn't the right word. And all these isolated sociological lines are a bit risky. And is the whistle too Britten-ish a 'trick'? It's odd how in a work of this sort even the tiniest actions seem to need considerable critical cogitation. It's probably not only just whether he's allowed to blow a whistle, but really is he allowed to be the means of a sort of momentary satyre on operatic methods, i.e. interrupt an ensemble by materialistic means? I am inclined to think that the slight elements of this attitude in the King Fisher-Bella-Ancients scene of Act I were sufficiently successful (& amusing) to be able to be tried again. And anything for some comic quality if possible, almost by any means. For you see where Papageno & P—— a can do a comic matrimonial duet – Jack & Bella, to be typical at all are sentimental & up against the housing shortage. The humour has to take a rather more 'Shavian' line. e.g. King Fisher's cloak etc.

I'm not sure that in the attempt to get variety in word rhythm the short lines of the Jack-Bella quarrel will come out right musically. I shall have to wait and see. But on the whole the words have been written to a fairly clear musical scheme. Most of it with settled key systems etc. . . .

Yrs.
Michael

Oxted   [31 August 1949]
Wed.

Dear Eric,

This draft script is one step further back than that of Act 2. i.e. it hasn't been reworked since 2 years or so – except that I've had notions which I've put down here or elsewhere. e.g. I can guess more clearly now what Sosostris sees in the bowl, from ancient ritualistic mystic marriages. But for Sosostris altogether I hope to get something from Valéry 'Charmes', 'La Pythie'. So that her aria will be still more personal, stressing her peculiar flesh & blood before she vanishes. This sort of process of deepening & pictorialising I find goes on unceasingly – while the music threatens to engulf it before it's completed. But if we waited for ever it'd never get done. Anyhow this Act 3 script is quite provisional with traces too of earlier discarded symbolisms – e.g. nets & fishing. I think now the re-veiling is a Veil dance pure & simple.

Till tomorrow –
Michael

At this point I seem to have made a suggestion that was of real help to the composer. The early draft of Act II referred to in this letter of 31 August started with four dances leading to an extended episode for Jack and Bella. I protested at this because I felt sure these dances would last longer than the estimate of '8–9 minutes' mentioned in his letter, and prove weightier and more significant than the usual set of operatic incidental dances, and their interpolation at this point might break the back of the opera if performed *in extenso*. I suggested therefore that the dances should be introduced so as to interrupt the Jack/Bella episode, and should themselves be interrupted after the third dance, leaving Jack and Bella free to resume and finish their scene. The fourth dance (the Fire Dance) could then be used to form the climax of Act III. The composer seemed to like this proposed re-arrangement.

Oxted   [10 September 1949]
Sat.

My dear Eric,

I'm quite sure this re-arrangement etc. is an improvement. The musical business of beginning with Strephon, breaking & then returning to the same point works out very well. Because the end of Jack's & Bella's lullaby runs beautifully into the preludial music to Strephon's dance etc. – with just Bella's & Jack's last '. . . wander deeper in the woods' coming pat over a long held horn bar. (It's for foreseeable musical reasons that I need them to kiss twice & speak twice.)

I'm pretty sure the interruption of the third dance & Bella's momentary hysterics & recovery works out well. With the empty stage for the last singing of all. So that we get a sort of meditation upon the stage presences.

I'm not quite so sure of the opening. I think Jack & Bella hiving off from the Chorus is probably the most natural way of getting them there – (rather than 2 separate entrances). And I'd like to keep Bella's proposal if I can – because in fact it is so true to type & in the scheme of the Interlude it fits nicely with the hunting of Strephon.

55

Either then I could make even more of the proposal i.e. having more &
subtler stops in the psychological process – or as it is – the minimum of
subterfuge, or 'delay', on Bella's part, before the announcement. (I hope
the verbal method to be used isn't too far-fetched. I've taken it,
because it once happened to me, by letter not on June 21st!, & it's the
only thing that came to mind.) The trouble comes as soon as Jack puts
practical objections, in order to give her some response. Because almost
any remark on those lines tends to destroy the idyllic character of the
Interlude. So I post you the latest compromise to see how it strikes an
outsider (?). But of course that really means I think that I'm hoping, now
that the characters are living people to you too, that you can help to test
their stage movements & words etc.

You'll see that I'm having to change the line 'Youth shld leap for
Age must fall' to suit the new scheme. The trouble with 'One must leap
& one must fall' is the equivocation of 'one' i.e., 'der Einer', or 'Man'.
It doesn't strike you & me so much that way for we've the original in
memory. Is 'he' & 'she' better? Or should the line be radically re-cast?

Then you'll see I've been able to describe the dances in rather more
detail.

The script of course is less representative in this 'Act' than ever.
Because the dances will be at least an 8 min touch I think – with
4 to 5 on either side. I can't quite gauge for the minute the duration
of the Chorus song. The first time you'll be able to disentangle from the
script the musical fact that I'm hearing now a sort of division of the
Chorus & half the song going on the way out of sight & half, after a
stage delay, going on fugally after it. So that we get as much as possible
the effect of depth to the wood.

Do you still feel it shld be Interlude, not Act 2? A minor point,
also: would it be helpful if the Act I were labelled? thus:

Act I. Morning. Interlude. Afternoon. Act 2. (Evening &) Night.
I'll perhaps ring you one evening, wh will be better than letter.

Yours.
Michael.

In a letter dated 12 September I suggested it was a mistake to refer
to Midsummer Day as '21 June'. I also made a few other suggestions,
which are referred to in the following letter. The discussion about a
revised text for the Jack/Bella scene was confirmed on the back of the
envelope where the composer wrote:

Wake up, wake up!
For I'm myself again.

Oxted
Wed.
                                          [14 September 1949]

Dear Eric,

What about an amended 'proposal' thus?:

                                          J.

B.   – But I can never guess.
Oh this time is quite different.
What day is it?

                                          Midsummer day.
Isn't that excuse enough?

                                          I've no idea.
Oh Jack, you're slow.
Is it Leap Year?

                                          You know the answer, Bella,
                                          Why ask me?

I feel as tho it should be.
For Jack you see, etc.

That removes 'June 21' & even gives Jack occasion to change from
good-humour to a slight bridle.

As to the Chorus Song. 'Hen' & 'Cock' won't really do, for the
latter has too literal a double sense. (No doubt the cock does fall in the
end!) So for the moment it better be 'she' & 'he'.

I like the idea of Jack falling. I first thought of Jack interfering
in the dance at Bella's instigation – but it seems too melodramatic. Next
I felt that Jack might accept Bella's intention to make-up with
resignation ('That will take no end of time') & lie down with his hands
behind his head to watch. When Bella comes to the 'Take a new look at
me' – he's asleep. Bella wakes him with something like:

                I'm quite myself again
                And if you want to keep me
                Catch me if you can.

Even this v. slight alteration *seems* to give a bit more importance to Jack.
He becomes less Bella's stage stooge (?) holding her mirror, & more
the long-suffering male, waiting for the partner to come out of the bath
room.

A v. slight alteration I want to the start. That Jack & Bella come
on first & the girls of the chorus final remark to run:

'They've led us off the track. Come on, or we shall lose the others.'
She's

I think this gives Bella's intention a slightly sharper definition. Also it

means that the chorus on the stage can have time to wheel round &
go back where they came & round behind. This is how the idea came to
me, because I need as much stage time as possible to hear what they
sing in their song before the 'distancing' starts.

I hadn't taken up the 'leap' & Leap Year. But I'd got George's
song in my head

> To the springing sap
> And the leaping life.

It's altogether quite a nice tie-up.

I've come across some fascinating allied stuff in a Yeats biography
(Norman Jeffares). Yeats equates the four elements to four (historical)
ages. (I'll show you his notes to the poem when you come.)

> He with body waged a fight
> Body won & walks upright.   (Earth)
>
> Then he struggled with the heart;
> Innocence & peace depart.   (Water)
>
> Then he struggled with the mind;
> His proud heart he left behind.   (Air)
>
> Now his wars with God begin;
> At stroke of midnight God shall win   (Fire).

It's the last couplet that's interesting – & Yeats' (similar) order.
In this connection have you any means to help me to 2 books (both
out of print)?

> Yeats   A Vision.   (Macmillan 1937)
> Cornford.   Thucydides Mythistorious

I have an idea there's a lot of stuff I need to see that might open more
doors. It's the matter of the Fire Dance & its relationship to the rest,
& to the 'reconciling symbol', the visionary transcendence – & the veils
& Strephon. There's still a tie-up which eludes us.

In a biography of St Joan I read yesterday the historical
material for the couplet

> Joan heard the voice first
> In father's garden at high noon.

I must break off.

Yrs.
Michael

The introduction mentioned in the next letter was not used. In the
latter part of this letter there is some gossip (here omitted) about the

current opera scene in London, which carries the first hint of a possible production of *The Midsummer Marriage* at the Royal Opera House, Covent Garden, where David Webster was general administrator and Peter Brook had recently been appointed artistic director.

Oxted   [23 November 1949]

My dear Eric,

That is as nothing to what I have lost in my time! Take heart therefore – probably even the heavenly files will 'slip up' – if that is not a horrid mixed metaphor. How else should most of us reach paradise!

I find that I wd have less in my collection of draft scripts than I expected. So I have only the original 'Handschrift' of the Introduction. (If you type a copy, then could you take a carbon & let me have).

I've never been certain yet whether this introduction is a good notion or not. I suppose it would help some & frighten others. It strikes me on re-reading that the end of it is not well done. That the more important idea of new techniques being offered us (& material) from the findings of anthropology, mythology & deep psychology, probably deserves a few sentences to itself. And that the Butcher quotation might be better transmuted into 'Tippett'. But it may be that it is really at all only stuff for an exterior monograph on the opera as I see it – & not to be printed with the text for ever. What do you think?

As to Act I. I think I shall write Tillett & ask him if his files can cough up a copy, & if he can put into it the corrections of those scenes he still has the score of. The corrections are so few, it is very little involved. And I will then put in what I've got. Then we should be getting near a definitive text at length.

I am coming off my hero's name. George increasingly worries me, because functionally & mythologically it's wrong. The hero is neither a farmer, nor yet does the name match Jenifer. Which is Cornish for Guinevere, as I expect you knew. But which also means probably 'The White Goddess' in some form. Anyhow white & feminine. I have been toying with the name Lance. Its disadvantage is that it's a diminutive & a bit precious. Yet it makes the high-falutin' pair quite separate nominally from the earth-bound lot.

Mythologically probably the name is Denis. But I'd like to have avoided a di-syllabic change in the existing music. Not that the name is in fact very often sung.

Goehr, on trying to formulate the story for the public, was arriving at something like this:

What is the opera about?

It's about a young couple who find they can't make a successful marriage without some preliminary unusual experiences, and another couple who find they can.

I am adopting that for the time being.

Goehr is sure that the possible cutting at rehearsal level in those few places where the music repeats can be left. He was surprised to find how un-padded it was. And, as I think I told you, he had a brain-wave for improving the second verse of King Fisher's aria – his dealings with the girls. I shall put that into practical composition sometime soon. But what Goehr hasn't seen yet are the scene between George (Lance) & Jenifer & the scene between K.F. & the Ancients. So he hasn't seen the most worked over scene of all – i.e. the quarrel of 'royal pair'. When he has seen the whole Act, we shall have another good judgment to add to our consensus gentium. . . .

Yours ever,
Michael

Oxted [30 December 1949]

My dear Eric,

All your nice letters, poems, type-scripts have caught me up, after my Christmas visiting of my Mother & John's mother. I can't criticize the poems because I'm not good enough. And probably the Greek element appeals to me very subjectively.

No – I didn't see 'The Cocktail Party' worse luck. Will it be published soon? I want to make a date with you in January if we may. Here or in London? Goehr does the Symphony with R.P.O. on Third Prog. Jan 21st (Hence our next concert as per leaflet – & G.'s generosity). So I might make a date in town on one of the days beforehand, when there's bound to be some pre-rehearsing. Or would you like another visit to the cottage? Could you say.

I'm hoping to finish Act 2 (Interlude) soon.

Yours
Michael

The first sentence of the next letter refers to a strange page of typing from my book *The Rise of English Opera*, where a gremlin seemed to have taken control of the keyboard.

Oxted   [15 January 1950]
Sunday

Dear Eric,

I was much intrigued by the stuttering type – trying indeed almost
to imitate Miss Stein (the elder). The whole page was quite tantalising.
I was relieved to know Berg spent 6 years on his great work, waiting
then 5 years for a performance! But I would like to have known the
climax of the crack at Wagner. Altogether I look forward to the book –
less concerning my own affairs indeed, but for the material & discussion
I imagine it will contain.

Incidentally, I'm thinking that 'chauffeur' is a bit out-of-date for
Jack, rather then what I call him – mechanic – despite the ever-living
'Enery Straker. What do you think?

I've been looking thro' the Dictionary of Christian Names. The
existing one-syllabled names are a mere handful – outside the
diminutives. The correct mythological name turns out to be Roy.
Anciently a Gaelic name, from 'Rhu' – red. But with modern
associations w. fr. Roi: (Jenifer is 'shimmering white', & a famous
Queen). Is it possible do you think to use Roy, despite the number of
horrid people of that name, in America & elsewhere?

I've had a stoppage for a week – but am back at it now again.
Haven't seen Webster yet tho.

Yrs.
Michael

Oxted   [February 1950]
Monday

Dear Eric,

Thanks a lot for the name-book. I'd actually read thro a later &
more authoritative dictionary, & your book does but confirm the
curious fact that single sounding names can be (outside the
diminutives) counted on the fingers. But I've been reading the
Mabinogion. There – unlike the principal double-names of the Anglo-
Saxons, Greeks & Latins – the single name proliferates. Lhyr (Lear),
Lhudd, Gwynn, Aedd, Math, Don etc. etc. And the last one strikes me
as possible. For Don is a good sounding name & Don was a divine-king
of some sort – probable Domus, Donar, a sky-god – connected with
rivers like Don, Donau, Rhone, & so on.

From another source (on Druidism) I've discovered that the Celtic
Fisher King had a truly wonderful name: Amangons. I do so much now

61

want to put him on the titles-page as Amangons alias King Fisher. I
think the right hero name will eventually come out of this celtic world.
I'm trying now to get hold of Cornish variants of the Welsh names –
like Jenifer herself. Also if Roy & Roe are derived from red, in Celtic –
maybe we can do a bit of linguistics & make a Cornish variant, when
I know the Cornish word for 'red' – & 'sky' & 'sun' & 'king' etc. etc.

Meanwhile the music goes on all the time & we're in sight of
the end of Act 2.

When Wilhelm Strecker comes back from New York in a week or so,
I'd like you to meet him, before he returns again to Mainz. Any
introduction ever you needed in Germany, he can provide. He will also
have just seen Stravinsky. I'll try & fix a lunch.

Till then –
Michael

I did not reply to the next letter, with its interesting suggestion, until
21 May; and then I told the composer I did not think I was the right
person to write the monograph he had in mind, mainly because I was
not sufficiently knowledgeable about deep psychology, anthropology,
and mythology.

The Windrose was a projected large-scale choral and orchestral
work, which never came to fruition.

Oxted   [18 March 1950]
Sat.

Dear Eric,

I enjoyed our lunch very much. Strecker was in unexpectedly good
form, & I revelled in the Stravinsky stories.

It was also very helpful from my point of view, as it cleared up my
mind as to what was possible & best for 'Midsummer Marriage'. I
suffered a mild crisis of fatigue afterwards, from which I'm slowly
recovering. Relief at the time delay, paradoxically mixed with anguish
at an apparently extending period of labour. Have I really gotten myself
into some utterly obscure and impossible imaginative world? – & are
not the struggles of composition defensive retardations of my better self,
rather than the supposed necessities of creating something within their
strange dual world of music and words?

Incidentally I do value my talks with you when they happen, just
because you have sympathy and knowledge of this dual world. For I

know that I must always return to it every so often, and for a big work. There is already the conception of a third work slowly germinating for an eventual birth years hence. A new choral & orchestral creation with a probable title of 'The Windrose'. But there's the opera to finish first!

But all these sort of stages in my creative life have some rhythm of their own also. Do you know – I've had a growing wish lately that you might, when at last 'The Midsummer Marriage' is delivered to the public, consider some monograph just upon the nature of this dual world, as it has forced itself upon me in 'A Child of Our Time' and the opera. For the method of using the emotional power of deep psychology, anthropology and mythology to fuse material into a collective contemporary work of art was used already in the oratorio. There is so much fascinating material to give anyone who had an inkling of what it might mean. Material which I think has more than a subjective interest, because it leads one immediately, without forethought of any sort, into the texture of our collective contemporary life.

And somewhere at the back of my mind is a dim unformulated notion of some new humanism – or fresh idea of the limits & quality of the human person – The Whole Man, as I call him. But that's too schematic probably. What I mean here in this letter is that any attempt to discuss this matter in criticism would be a very great positive step. Least that is how it seems to me. Because it's not one person, or even one art, or the creators alone, or the therapists or the mystics or the 'grim & gay' nonchalant youth – so that *should* it come to some attempted formulation in criticism *too*, then we have all gained. Even if supercession will be the fate of creator & critic alike. But maybe I'm talking nonsense and it isn't your line anyhow. Just a dream Faber book . . .!

Much love to you both.

I must come to see you soon.

Michael

Perhaps the gulf in England between music (or at any rate the music critics) & the general world of ideas, art & literature etc. is too wide to be bridged, & that any attempt would drop into the gulf and smash. Or is there somewhere after all a different public that lives in a less partitioned world, if admittedly such a public is yet small? and probably mostly, in music, catered for thru radio? But if there is no such joining of hands, then why am I driven on this road with such command? Why – to bring it to the concrete – am I asked to speak to the annual Conference of The Guild of Pastoral Psychology? – *even* tho a musician!!

Is it just a fatal dissipation of energies or a sign of a wider net & a deeper throw? If I take another sheet of paper I feel in my bones I shall end by quoting Goethe . . . .

Oxted   [22 May 1950]
Monday

My dear Eric,

Thanks for your letter. I had given thought to the matter you raise for Act 2, & it has solved itself differently – or rather the intermediary world has come about by other means. At the start of the Act you have preludial music which leads direct to Strephon alone on the stage & even to his first steps – & the first operatic-vocal music comes from out of the distance off-stage. So that the operatic world appears like an interruption & only bit by bit do you forget the first world, during the development of the scene between Jack & Bella. But their duet ends in an embrace which is musically the Prelude di nuovo & this music is then felt as two things e.g. the love of J. & Bella – their 'walk to the paradise garden' – & they cross the stage in a dream-like slow 'dance' – & as they go out of stage focus, Strephon appears again in his place, doing precisely the same movement & poses, of which you have seen a taste before. But they go further this time, in a kind of preludial solo dance wh is not v. rhythmic – but wh stops abruptly, to allow the shimmer of the celesta. . . .

The composer was taken ill at the end of May.

[postcard]

Aldeburgh   [June 1950]
Tues.

Regaining strength rapidly now. Look very different in colour.

Think I can manage end of Act 2 without a messenger. Same notion but more within the 'idyll', so that transition to the final silent stage will be easier.

M.

In my letter of 21 May I had mentioned various books by Adrian Stokes which I had been reading with enjoyment, particularly *Stones*

THE MIDSUMMER MARRIAGE. *Above:* The Welsh National Opera production (1977), showing Felicity Lott as Jennifer and John Treleavan as Mark (*Sheppard*). *Below:* Act I of the production of the State Opera of South Australia, as seen at the Adelaide Festival of Arts, 1978. *Inset:* Arthur Davies as Jack and Mary Davies as Bella in the Welsh National Opera production (*Sheppard*)

KING PRIAM: setting by Sean Kenny. Act III. Helen (Margreta Elkins) protests her innocence to Andromache (Josephine Veasey, left) and Hecuba (Marie Collier, right) (*Wilson*)

KING PRIAM. *Above:* Troy at war. *Below:* Priam (Forbes Robinson) begs Achilles
(Richard Lewis) to hand over the body of his son Hector (Victor Godfrey)
(*Rogers*)

THE KNOT GARDEN. *Above:* Act I, design by Timothy O'Brien, production by Peter Hall (*Robinson*). *Below:* Mel and Dov do their 'act' with Flora (Jill Gomez) as audience (*Dominic*)

THE KNOT GARDEN. *Above:* Dov (Robert Tear) kisses Faber (Raimund Herincx)
while Mel (Thomas Carey) looks on and Mangus (Thomas Hemsley) observes the
scene from a distance (*Robinson*)

THE ICE BREAK: production by Sam Wanamaker at Covent Garden, 1977.
This page above: Olympion (Clyde Walker) arrives at the airport lounge.
Below: Olympion and Hannah (Beverley Vaughn), Act II.
Opposite above: Tribalization of the black and white mobs, Act II.
Below: Yuri's operation, Act III (*Dominic*)

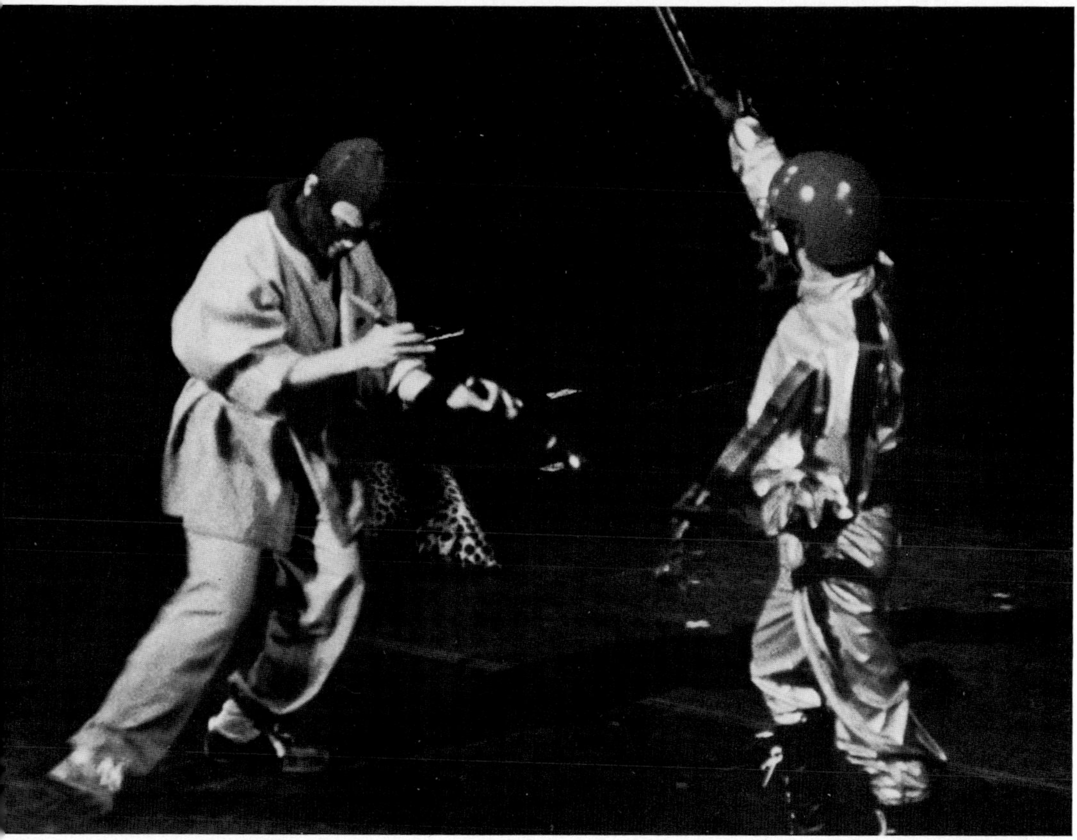

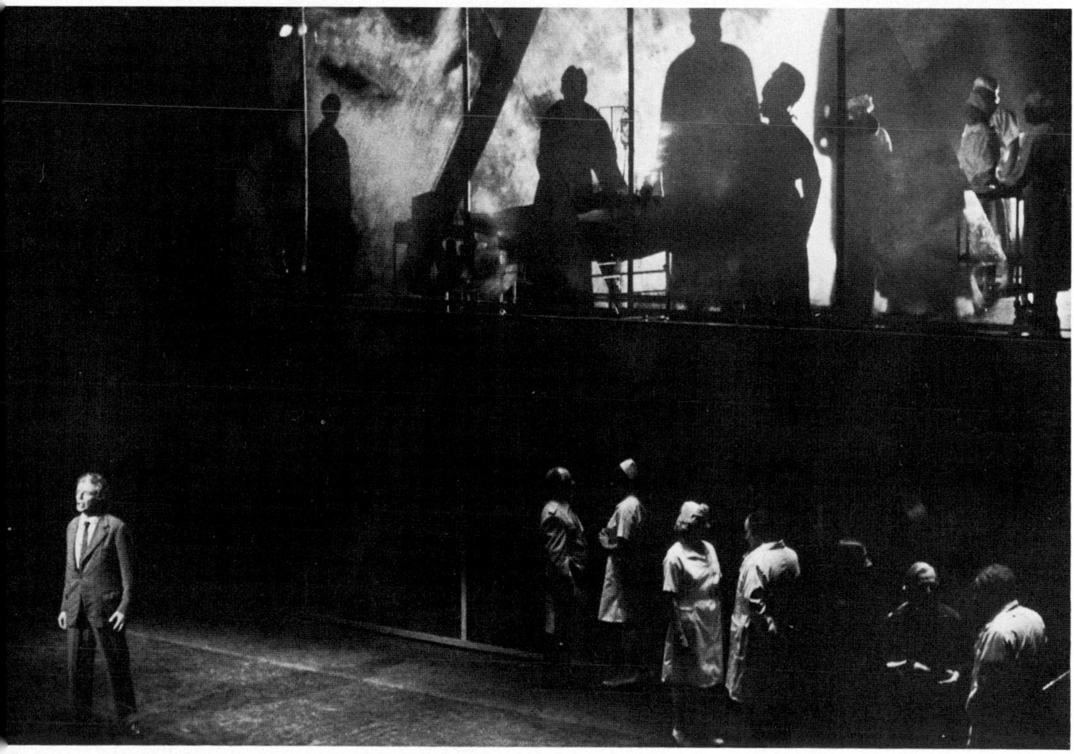

THE ICE BREAK: production at the Opernhaus, Kiel, June 1978. *Above:* General stage set (*Thode*). *Below:* Yuri is wheeled away from the operating theatre (*Thode*)

of Rimini and *Colour and Form*. KK is intended for Sir Kenneth Clark. –
later Lord Clark.

Oxted   [14 September 1950]

My dear Eric,

You wrote me in May last (when I was ill) about a letter I'd
written you 2 months before. So this letter is at about the same rate of
correspondence! It's the matter of a monograph on the 'dual world', as
I name it, of the work I'm at present busy with, & of 'A Child of Our
Time' which has seemed to me (at one time) or another) worthy of
consideration. Because, on these occasions, when an artist is forced well
below the surface to produce a fusion of experience wherein many
disparate things are in some way transmuted & crystalised, an artistic
process happens which is, despite its regular appearance in the past,
perhaps specially demanded by the fragmentation of the age in which we
live.

What you wrote in May has only lately come clear to me. Because
I hadn't read Adrian Stokes' books, and analogies to painters is less my
main line of country. But it now seems to me that this is in itself
stimulating & valuable – & is a line of country which (independently of
your suggestion) I have been beginning to explore. (In particular some
remarks of K.K., in his book of landscape paintings about light in
certain pictures, being a unifying, almost tangible medium, gave me a
most exact analogy & therewith assistance to something that I hope to
do in the opera. And this strikes me now as similar to your remarks à
propos Piero della Francesca & Cézanne.) So if you're still interested in
these speculations, & not as yet too immersed in anything else, would
you like some meeting to talk?

At present the end of Act 2 is flowing out at a good pace & I'm
getting rather excited by the anticipatory feeling of another great chunk
completed. This means that I'm a bit chary of too long a gap. But,
as my new way of life has so markedly curtailed my extra-compositorial
interests & duties, I can take time (that is a day or 24 hours) off to suit
myself – & with advantage. I haven't quite yet discovered how much
time & how often – but clearly I can't go on 7 days a week without
some break. So every week I take some day off somewhere, more or less.

Would you like to come down here a night? Or week-end? There's
no hurry. And in any case you may have put the whole idea out of your
head.

Yours ever
Michael

Oxted   [November 1950]
Tues.

My dear Eric,

I'm sending you the revised draft of the opening of Act 3, & an old script (please don't lose!) of Act I, so that you can see what went before. It may materially affect the tiny opening preamble between Ancients & K. Fisher, for they have a longer go in Act I. I've put a pencil query against that. Otherwise there's another query against the end of their scene.

What I'm first of all needing is an O.K. for the very opening because the music has begun & after Christmas the opening words will begin to be submerged, willy nilly.

Secondly, I want to discuss Sosostris' opening gambits for her Aria, Monologue or whatever, because it's there I am stuck. (Quite a lot of stuff later on I have already improved.) Thirdly, the scene in Act I between Jack, Bella & K.F. & chorus is v. relevant to the scene in Act 3 between ditto & Ancients, as to what Jack will choose. I think because of Act I we can't have Jack silent between Bella & K.F. because that's already been done. I don't think I'm really happy with my proposed Jack (silent) defended by Bella against K.F. I still feel that the solution may be as I have it Jack & Bella, Ancients, Chorus, King Fisher (aside), but less to do with the young couple's comfort & urges, as Bella's fears of the uncanny, the sacrilege of doing what K.F. orders. The ensemble might then be: Jack still not quite convinced, Bella convinced – Ancients on sacrilege in general – Chorus willing to let Jack & Bella choose for them – King Fisher savouring the emotion of pride – out of which comes Jack's choice. If this is so it would help if one saw roughly how the stage would be. I wanted Jack & Bella to draw apart into the bosom of the whole chorus so that they make a group – while K.F. is solo as 'Anti-God', & the Ancients may even come on to main stage level, so as not to space out the ensemble too much. And when J. & B. eventually go off, I wanted the Chorus to sweep over the stage to sing their good-bye – wh can well be the end of their Act 2 song, sung just as remembrance: 'She must leap & he must follow' – which by irony becomes significant for the scene to follow – Sosostris leaps (into thin air!) & K.F. falls – dead.

I'll ring you quite soon – about all this. If you know of anyone wanting a bungalow in the country its going on sale now. To a private buyer £2,500. (The Agents have put too high a price on it). I think it will go quite quickly.

                                          Yours
                                          Michael

Have I gone too far into the farcical element of the chorus bringing
in the false Sosostris, 'The Sphinx & the Sibyl rolled in one'? Certainly
in general opera benefits by sharp contrasts & less mixtures. A farcical
pseudo-Sosostris to throw into relief the real thing.

The song-cycle here mentioned was *The Heart's Assurance*, a setting of
poems by Sydney Keyes and Alun Lewis for high voice and piano.
Its first performance was given by Peter Pears and Benjamin Britten at
the Wigmore Hall on 7 May 1951.

Tidebrook   [4 April 1951]
Wed.

My dear Eric,

Your p.c. comes as I have just finished the song cycle & am
collecting myself together for Act 3 Scene 2. (Sc. 1 is finished). So the
old question of the text returns to plague us. But you have not seen the
much amended version beyond the first pages, which you should not
have lost this time! You suggested then to have the drunken man sing
solo, & a dancing-man answer. And that has been managed v. successfully.
So that the 1st choric 'Ode' has come off well & steers us nicely from
jollification to 'night' – with touches of [?] at the end out of which
the 2nd choric 'Ode' ("Even in a summer night") will come, after the
big climax. King Fisher has entered the stage – & that is where I am.
All that's missing from the enclosed is the v. end, which I've recast
again (Jack & Bella once more *not* returning). It went this morning to a
typist. It's only about a page. But it's an annoying page – tho I hope it's
come right this time. . . .

Première of Songs is Wigmore – May 7. Come if you can. On p. 9
of the script it appears to me that Sos. sees the lion too soon. It needs
another step on the way & another K.F. interjection. So that he begins
'Jenifer!' (no more) & ends 'Mark!' – no less.

dein
Michael

Tidebrook   [30 March 1952]
Sun.

My dear Eric,

I was afraid it was an awful long time since we communicated.
Yes – the second dawn 'commence à pointer', Jack & Bella have just
left the stage for good. In 3 weeks Sosostris will vanish & King Fisher

die. Then (Ap 20) I have a 5 day break, before the last 3 months & last 3 scenes. All of which have been better modelled now. I got a lot of good material out of an illustrated book on Indian religious art by Zimmer.

And now – what about a visit here – à 1, à 2 – or even if you needed à 3. You wld be welcome. Just let me know.

I saw 'Wozzeck' – but was twice ill before 'Budd'. Are you going these next times? If so, p'raps I might accompany you & repay my way to you?

à bientot
Michael

Tidebrook   [summer 1952]
Tuesday

Dear Eric,

The enclosed is the v. end of all: in its latest form. Musically – the 'bird-song' & the dawn lead to a kind of echo of Act I early morning, & the flute calls lead to the voices off, out of wh the whole opera started. The 'Hulloa!'s echo too – but without formal repetition. (All is different if the same). Then Mark enters as tho he were finishing his Love Song (of Act I) afresh, and this time Jenifer is dressed aright. Their epigrams refer to their initial disagreements, re love & truth, as values. Something of that kind there must be. – either verbally or visually or dramatically – but I'm disinclined for any long scene & consequent anti-climax. So it's pared to the bones – & it will be but a minute before Mark turns his young back on the Ancients & the 'other world' – & the 'Comoedia' in the strict old sense begins.

Till Tuesday evening next.
Michael

The 'string piece' for the Edinburgh Festival mentioned in the next letter was the *Fantasia Concertante on a Theme of Corelli*.

Tidebrook   [15 August 1952]
Fri.

My dear Eric,

It wld have been more than nice to see you but – I'm on holiday in Ticino, Switz. from Monday for 3 weeks. . . .

68

Meanwhile the last notes will be written between Sept 10 &
Oct 1 – so far as I can see – with full score up to the last bar. Also
John has helped to get the 'Ritual Dances' from 'The M.M.' off in score
to Mainz, where they will print immediately, for the 'création' is at Bâle
on Feb 13, by Sacher (English première under Goehr, B.B.C., in
March).

There is no rest for the wicked, for I have accepted a commission
to write a string piece for Edinburgh Festival next year (Still
confidential).

Karajan does the 'Child' in Italy in the winter, & we've been busy
printing an Italian version. Possibly also later in Vienna. So all is v.
active. Almost too active.

The last Act has turned out really well & in excellent & clear
shape. I feel in no hurry to present it. It's a huge piece of imagination &
should not be hurried on to the stage. I am quite content to let the
'Ritual Dances' make their point first. . . .

Act 3 did have to get even further cleared up & simplified. You
will be interested, having seen earlier drafts.

I know Morar well. A deep blue, black, green, cold Loch. I've
camped on its edge (with John) & broken camp to hike slowly up to
Gairloch. *Very* romantic! They've much improved the surface of The
Road to the Isles since I first travelled on it.

And now to my own holiday.

> Love to you all
> Michael

P.S. Come to Tidebrook tho soon, please.

The following letter refers to a lecture on Poetic Drama and the
Opera that Tippett had been invited to deliver to a course on twentieth-century English literature organised by the British Council and
the Board of Extra-Mural Studies of the University of Cambridge.
He was too busy to undertake this commission, so by general consent
the invitation was transferred to me, and I delivered the lecture at
Madingley Hall on 6 July 1953.

'A new longer work' probably refers to the Concerto for Piano
and Orchestra.

Tidebrook   [received 16 July 1953]
Wed.

Dear Eric,

 Many thanks for letting me see the lecture in draft. Seems a lot of
good material – & am glad it provoked interested discussion.

 Shan't make the 21st (leider!) because I have to be in town all
20th, & probably 24th, so it's too much in a week. And I've begun,
slowly, a new longer work. Meanwhile Covent Garden seems to have
plonked for January 55, & no previous English broadcast. Any
previous continental première of course can't be prevented.

 This news is v. new & probably not official. I thought you'd be
glad to know it.

herzlichst
Michael

Shortly after the premiere, I wrote the composer an enthusiastic letter
about his triumph, in which I made a number of comments on matters
of production. Among other points, I told him I had found myself
hankering after a pistol shot at the moment of King Fisher's death.

Tidebrook   [3 February 1955]
Thurs.

My dear Eric,

 Glad it came across to you. I've had such moving accounts from
people of quite different approach. The magic really seems to have
worked. Walton himself quite overenthusiastic abt the music – & 'unter
Kollegen' that means a lot. I shd like to talk to you later abt it again.
A school of thought wants me to cut the v. end; viz the return to earth
of the divine couple, & leave them at the end of Fire Dance in their
apotheosis. This so alters my original conception that I'm frightened of it.
Maybe it's just that the magnificent Hepworth sets doesn't allow of any
recession of the visual – magical at the v. end, as I described it in the
text.

 I won't be driven into anything so drastic till I have taken quiet
stock. I'm more inclined to try & pull the last set a bit together here &
there, & especially the 'cold' bit before the 2nd dawn. Giving just long
enough for the pair to change. Maybe the pistol shot is right. I always
used to have it. Let me know anything you think.

Yours
Michael

En route for Tidebrook   [23 February 1955]
Wed.

Dear Eric,

Sorry not to have answered before – & to say yes to your requests.
Might I be allowed to have a glance at the chapter in proof? I mean,
simply because so much seems to depend now on getting thro to good
sense & facts. Tho I'm sure you will do all that!

I saw the Zürcher Zeitung in Switzerland. Cld you lend your
copy to Schotts? Have just been recording a dialogue on it all in Italian
– for R.A.I.

Train is going too fast to write in.

Herzlichst
Michael

'... the chapter in proof' refers to an article on *The Midsummer
Marriage* that I was writing for the *Adelphi*.

The notice in the *Neue Zürcher Zeitung* was written by my friend,
Dr Martin Hürlimann of Atlantis Verlag, who had attended the
first night at Covent Garden.

Tidebrook   [25 February 1955]
Fri.

Dear Eric,

I'd written yesterday to D.W. saying almost exactly what you've
written. That, in *my* opinion, to cut out chunks of music will only *add*
to incoherency, until we have wrestled with confusions that have come
about theatrically. (Particularly the damping of the drama between
Sosostris & K.F.) I am prepared to cut of course if needed, but I am
saying I can't & won't do it unless it is decided on (by us all so to speak)
within the total production. So I am asking for a long session with Ch.
West before I do anything at all. Yesterday, for the first time, I became
suddenly clear that this was an absolute. In any case it's only a matter of
some small cuts I want myself. I refuse to rewrite anything yet – if ever!
But I need first & foremost a stocktaking of where & how & why a
sense of obscurity supervenes – & then to see whether it can't be
removed by production. Because *on the air*, for example, Act 3 sounds
the best of all – admirably balanced. Wld like to talk sometime. Am off
to Dortmund tomorrow for my old symphony.

Love.
M.

The seven-year stint of projecting, drafting and composing *The Midsummer Marriage* came to an end late in 1952. In the two subsequent years it was largely a matter of discussing details of production. This was a field that was new to Tippett. He had never worked in a theatre before; and some of the last letters in the correspondence here printed show that he was becoming aware of the important part stage production could play in helping this opera – or any other opera of his – to make its proper operatic effect.

The production at Covent Garden was entrusted to the house producer, Christopher West. At first it was agreed to invite Ben Nicolson to design the scenery and costumes; but after some thought he decided he was unable to accept, and the invitation was transferred to his wife, Barbara Hepworth, the sculptress, who had recently designed an impressive production of *Electra* at the Old Vic.

Despite the risk of a certain measure of duplication between the draft material as discussed by the composer in his letters to me and the definitive version as it appears in the engraved score and the printed libretto, it seemed worthwhile here to summarize the action in its final form.

The first pair of lovers – the 'royal' pair – is named Mark and Jenifer. Mark is a young man of mysterious antecedents, ignorant of the secret of his birth. Jenifer is the daughter of King Fisher, a rich businessman with strong views about her eventual marriage, and Mark is not the sort of man he wants as son-in-law. Nevertheless, Jenifer has made up her mind to elope with Mark; their rendezvous is a clearing in a wood at the top of a hill; and the time, just after dawn on midsummer day. The stage is set for their Midsummer Marriage.

They meet: but Mark to his dismay finds Jenifer has changed her mind. Not that she has any intention of returning to her father; but she wishes to break away from the material world and experience what she calls 'truth'. Seeing a flight of broken steps on the hill-top, she ascends these and disappears from view, while the disappointed Mark descends through gates into a cave below. King Fisher appears, and his attempt to bribe the members of the chorus to help him in his search for Jenifer is not successful. Jenifer and Mark return and describe their experiences in heaven and hades respectively in two big arias – Jenifer's having coloratura and Mark's being rhapsodic.

If the action of *The Midsummer Marriage* was to be confined to 'one place and one time', there remained a gap between the moment (end of Act I) when Mark and Jenifer leave the stage to complete the second part of their various progresses and their reappearance transfigured at the climax of Act III. This gap Tippett decided to treat as a kind of interlude, filling it partly with the courtship of his second pair of lovers (Jack and Bella) and partly with a set of incidental dances for the dancers belonging to the supernatural world (Act II).

In the case of Jack and Bella, it is the woman who is the dominant partner. When Jack the mechanic first appears in Act I and sings his opening aria, 'Like every working man I know how best to do my single job', Bella cannot keep quiet, but joins in as soon as he refers to his dreams, and what began as a solo finishes as a duet. In Act II it is Bella who, finding Jack a little too slow for her liking, takes advantage of the fact that it is Leap Year to tell him she's made up her mind to throw up her job as King Fisher's secretary and marry him. They will settle down in a house of their own, she says, and rear a family. Jack is quite content to follow her lead; and in Act III when King Fisher orders him to unveil Sosostris, it is Bella who sees that such a gesture is tantamount to sacrilege and urges her lover to break away from subservience to a fascist master while there is still time. All the way through, the motive power that drives her forward is biological; and at the moment of crisis she knows instinctively that the time has come 'for the unborn child to speak'.

The supernatural element in the opera consists of two Shavian Ancients (a priest and priestess) who inhabit a kind of temple or sanctuary on the hilltop, and a group of neophytes. The He-Ancient and She-Ancient play no direct part in the action, but act as chorus-leaders, bringing a hieratic solemnity to the scenes on which they comment. The neophytes are dancers. They take part in certain ceremonial moments in Act I: but their great opportunity comes in Act II, when the focus of the opera shifts in the drowsy midsummer afternoon from the vocal expression of the humans to the dance ritual of the silent supernatural world. In sympathy with this change of focus, the scenery is slewed to the right; and this new slant gives the action and the argument behind the action a kind of stereoscopic depth.

In the four Ritual Dances (the earth in autumn, the waters in winter; the air in spring; and fire in summer) the dancers become spirits of natural phenomena. The first three dances are dramas of pursuit: a hare chased by a hound, a fish hunted by an otter, a bird struck down by a hawk. In each case it is the male who is pursued by the female; and the implication is that the fulfilment of the female causes the death of the male. Bella, who oversees the third dance, watches it 'with increasing fascination and horror . . . not knowing if what she sees is real or her own dreams'. Her involuntary scream interrupts the dance sequence, which is resumed and completed in the midnight Fire Dance at the climax of Act III, when the trans-figured Mark and Jenifer are withdrawn into the heart of the flames as a voluntary human sacrifice – a climax that brings to mind the close of Eliot's *Four Quartets*:

And all shall be well and
All manner of thing shall be well
When the tongues of flame are in-folded
Into the crowned knot of fire
And the fire and the rose are one.

There are several passages in *The Midsummer Marriage* where Tippett's indebtedness to Eliot is apparent. Mark on his return journey from the underworld (Act I) sings of his experiences 'rocked in a boat across the water coldly lapping the waste land'. Eliot's notes to *The Waste Land* explicitly refer to the Fisher King chapter in Jessie L. Weston's *From Ritual to Romance*; and possibly this may also be the source of Tippett's big business man, 'King' Fisher. In the opening section of *The Waste Land* we are also introduced to 'Madam Sosostris, famous clairvoyante' and her 'wicked pack of cards'; and this is the original of Tippett's Sosostris, the clairvoyante who is 'a medium not an end'.

At the beginning of the opera King Fisher is shown trying to exercise parental control over Jenifer and prevent what he considers to be a thoroughly undesirable runaway marriage. But Jenifer has already revolted against her father before the curtain rises; and all King Fisher can do is to try to use hirelings to achieve his aims. He wants the gates leading to the cave opened because he thinks his daughter is detained inside; but when persuasion fails, he decides to use force, and Jack is hired to do the job. Always using others to do his work for him if possible, King Fisher is hopelessly at a loss when confronted by the supernatural and finds direct communication impossible. His daughter has escaped from his sphere of influence to some place where apparently he cannot follow her: so, to discover her whereabouts and to get in touch with her again, he needs the services of a clairvoyante and summons Madam Sosostris. But when the truth begins to shine through as a result of her divination, it proves unpalatable and his disbelief immediately strikes her dumb. In anger he orders her to be exposed, but his henchman, Jack, refuses to obey his orders, and he is forced to take direct action himself. This results in the disclosure of Mark and Jenifer transfigured – in the Hindu pose of perpetual copulation. In desperation, King Fisher tries to free Jenifer by shooting Mark but the folly of this act recoils on him, and he falls dead himself.

Sosostris makes but one appearance in the opera (in Act III), though her warning voice is heard off-stage for a few bars in Act I. The voice is an alto, and it issues from 'a huge contraption of black veils of roughly human shape, though much more than life-size'. In true pythian tradition, the face (or any approximation thereto) is invisible. No lips are seen to move, so the words issuing from the oracle are difficult to apprehend. Sosostris's single aria in Act III consists of four gradually expanding sections. It starts slowly, and with a low vocal tessitura, but as it progresses, each section moves rather more quickly and is pitched higher than the preceding one, and so the message becomes increasingly urgent. In the initial section, she warns her listeners that 'the illusion that you practise power is delusion'; in the second, she laments her forgotten and forbidden womanhood and the fact that she alone cannot consult herself; and the third is an exhortation to eschew disbelief – one of the simplest and most radiantly beautiful and moving moments of the opera. *Sunt lacrimae rerum*! At that point her aria becomes narrative and describes the ancient ritual of the Divine Marriage applied to Mark and Jenifer as she sees it disclosed on the crystal bowl.

There is nothing especially difficult or obscure about the action of this opera, or these characters, once one is prepared to accept the fact that *The Midsummer Marriage* is a statement in natural and supernatural terms of the struggle between the sexes before carnal love 'becomes transfigured as divine'. All this is presented with classical economy, and in conformity with the rules of the three unities. The wonder is that Tippett not only worked out an extremely rich and exciting libretto, but also clothed it with music of surpassing beauty and invention. In retrospect it seemed extraordinary that a sensitive and committed musician, whose life had been affected by the bitter years of economic depression in the early 1930s, who had lived through the tragic outbreak of the Spanish Civil War and watched the Nazi menace grow darker and grimmer in Central Europe, and then found himself caught up in a war, which he did not approve of, but could not altogether avoid, should have produced so rich and generous an opera score, redolent of hope, happiness, optimism, and displaying an irresistible lyricism.

There are several vocal highlights in the opera. Sosostris's aria has already been mentioned. Mark's rhapsodic air at the opening of Act I, 'Ah! the summer morning dances in my heart', has an ecstatically happy rising vocal line, analogous to the lark's song. Jenifer's song, when she returns to earth towards the end of Act I, 'Sweet was the peace', is radiant with transcendental splendour, and as she recalls how her soul left her body when she joined in the dance of the congregation of the stars, her vocal line rises and its tessitura becomes increasingly exposed, until it reaches a point where it is accompanied only by a trumpet *dolcissimo e leggiero* – a brilliant two-part invention like a dangerous tight-rope act with no safety-net.

This passage is repeated, not literally, but subject to certain changes and developments, e.g. it modulates a tone higher. Similar examples can be found elsewhere in the score, with the result that the musical argument is generally being carried a stage forward at the same time as the musical form is being consolidated. Even when, as in King Fisher's aria with its two stanzas, one addressed to the male members of the chorus, and the other to the women, it looks as if the musical form is going to be built on *da capo* lines, literal repetition is avoided and the second stanza is varied so that it leads in a different musical direction.

The choruses in *The Midsummer Marriage* are particularly varied and challenging – in fact, no other opera of Tippett's makes such extensive demands on the chorus. At the beginning of the opera it is the members of the chorus, who, gathering on the hilltop. carry the audience rapidly into the excitement of sunrise on Midsummer Day and the rest of the action that follows. In one or two places there are what might be called 'distancing' choruses. This is particularly the case in Act II, where the full chorus is wandering through the woods, and fragments of their song, 'In the summer season on the longest day of all', are heard off-stage at the beginning and end of this act. Act III opens with a magnificent chorus celebrating sundown and the White Goddess's journey to the west at night. After King Fisher breaks Sosostris's bowl, a big ensemble of perplexity is built up, consisting of Bella trying to persuade Jack to disobey his master, Jack gradually succumbing to her argument, King Fisher unwilling to abdicate one jot of his power, the two Ancients commenting on the mystery of free-will, and the chorus sympathising in general terms with Jack and Bella.

The rhythmic elasticity of the score is remarkable. Certain aspects of it derive from the madrigalian technique that Tippett first used in his second String Quartet, 'where each part may have its own rhythm and the music is propelled by the differing accents, which tend to thrust each other forward'. Sometimes, as in the opening of Act III, the effect is reminiscent of the compound folk tunes and dance rhythms of the Balkans. A curious cumulative procedure can be observed in the third Ritual Dance where the time signature of the spring dance of the tree leaves, which is 6/8 at its first appearance, becomes 7/8 at its second and 8/8 at its third and final appearances. Another passage deserving attention because of its metrical richness is the coda to the opera where a final instrumental chorale of thanks-giving is accompanied by seven great isolated breakers of orchestral sound made out of 3-bar units, each containing separate but syn-chronised 6/4, 9/4, and 27/8 metrical strands.

A lush harmonic richness is to be found in much of the score; and in certain passages enharmonic ambivalence is a directional pointing to the natural and sometimes to the supernatural order of things. This is particularly the case in Act II, with the setting of the stage for the Ritual Dances. The muted horn cadence at the end of the act is an especially emotive enharmonic device.

The intensity of Tippett's visual imagination when creating *The Midsummer Marriage* is reflected in the detailed care with which he filled out the stage directions. The description of the stage, the main features of which are crucial to the action, is as follows:*

When fully lighted the stage, as seen from the audience, presents a clearing in a wood, perhaps at the top of a hill, against the sky. At the back of the stage is an architectural group of buildings, a kind of sanctuary, whose centre appears to be an ancient Greek temple. The stage in front of the temple and within the whole semi-circular group of buildings is raised, with steps leading down to the lower level of the main stage. To the right, as one faces the temple, these steps end in an ascending spiral stone staircase, which seems to break abruptly in mid-air. . . . To the left, the steps lead further down through gates into the hillside itself, for the gates look like the entrance to a cave. . . . While the sky-line is clear behind the temple, the trees of the wood seem almost to mix with the other buildings, and are plentiful (in the wings) on the lower stage as well.

*Taken from the section headed NOTAE in the score and libretto.

At the beginning of Act I, mist rises from the buildings after sunrise. In Act II the scene takes a turn to the right. In Act III it is back again as in Act I; but when the night is over and dawn comes, it is seen that the temple and sanctuary have disappeared in the morning mist.

Another section that carries a plethora of stage directions is the Ritual Dances, where the dancers' action is described in close detail. There is a curious passage which perhaps deserves special mention. This comes at the beginning of the third dance, 'The Air in Spring', where the dancers sow a field of spring corn, moving right across the stage and returning. At this point the composer decided to incorporate a gratuitous act. The following direction has been retained in his score – *They throw a handful of corn for luck, down stage right* – but it has been deleted from the libretto.

It is as if the composer was doing everything he could to reassure himself that the stage action was viable, since he saw it and described it with such intensity, but it must be admitted that the original production may have suffered from this emphasis. The Barbara Hepworth decor was handsome and haunting, but it turned out to be heavy and awkward to handle on the stage, and did not seem to leave sufficient space for the movements of the chorus and dancers. Subsequent productions have moved away from realism and a literal interpretation of the composer's directions and concentrated more on lighting effects, colour, and design.

The original production was under the musical direction of John Pritchard. Jenifer and Mark were sung by Joan Sutherland and Richard Lewis; the second pair of lovers by Adele Leigh and John Lanigan. Otakar Kraus was King Fisher, and Oralia Dominguez, Sosostris. The choreography was by John Cranko. After an initial run of five performances at Covent Garden, this production was revived for three performances during the 1956–7 season. (In the event, owing to the illness of some members of the cast, only two of these scheduled performances took place.) At that point of time, one might have had to admit that the opera had not yet succeeded in establishing itself; but in 1963 an important thing happened. Norman del Mar conducted a studio performance for the B.B.C, in conditions which revealed the full magnificence of the score. No one who heard that performance could have doubted that here was one of the masterpieces of twentieth-century music. Five years later Covent Garden decided to mount an entirely new production under the musical direction of Colin Davis. The producer was Ande Anderson, and the designer Tony Walton. This was given at the Royal Opera House on 10 April 1968 and had a run of six performances during the season. After this triumphant revival, the composer remarked, 'Yet the creation did take place in complete obscurity many years ago and was a prolonged act of faith such as we may not accomplish twice in a lifetime.'

The new production was revived for three performances in July 1970. The cast of this 1970 revival was used for the recording of the opera under Colin Davis made by Philips the same year, which was awarded the Grand Prix du Disque de l'Académie Charles Cros in 1972.

It cannot be said that the first German production, given in the Badisches Staatstheater, Karlsruhe, on 29 September 1973 was an unqualified success. But a marked change came over the scene three years later when the Welsh National Opera decided to mount it in Cardiff (22 September 1976) and send it on tour in England. The music director was Richard Armstrong. The production was in the hands of Ian Watt Smith. The choreography was by Terry Gilbert. Ralph Koltai supplied the decor, and Annena Stubbs the costumes. How successfully it worked out could be seen from David Cairns's review in *The Sunday Times* of 26 September 1976, where he praised the dedication and intelligence of the Welsh National Opera and hailed the production as a 'triumph of teamwork', going on to say:

and the result is to make the opera, for the first time in the theatre, an integrated work of art, a coherent dramatic experience, in which music, text, declamation, solo and choral song, lighting, gesture, mime, dance are fused into a composite language of expressive power. Played, sung, acted and danced like this (and experienced for the first time in a smallish theatre) *The Midsummer Marriage* throws off the awkwardness and confusions that seemed once to encumber its beauties; it becomes, with all its complexity of allusions and intertwining metaphors, a work of marvellous directness, fresh, unhampered, and young.

It was this production that the Welsh National Opera took with it to Portugal, when it gave two performances of *The Midsummer Marriage* at the Teatro Nacional de São Carlos, Lisbon, in February 1979.

A similar success was enjoyed by the State Opera of South Australia when on 25 February 1978 it produced *The Midsummer Marriage* as part of the Adelaide Festival of the Arts. There was never any doubt about the impact of the work on the Australian audience which came to it fresh and with open minds. It was a triumph. The musical director was Myer Fredman, the producer Adrian Slack, and the choreographer Jonathan Taylor. The designs were by John Cervenka.

A handsome edition of the full score limited to 200 copies was published by Schott's in 1975. The pencil manuscript of the score was acquired by the British Library in the 1960s, but with the exception of one detached leaf which has survived on its own, the ink manuscript disappeared shortly after the score was engraved and has not yet reappeared.

THE MIDSUMMER MARRIAGE

First performed 27 January 1955
Royal Opera House, Covent Garden

Opera in three acts.
Words and Music by Michael Tippett

STREPHON, *one of the dancers*	Pirmin Trecu
THE ANCIENTS, *priest and priestess of the Temple*	Michael Langdon
	Edith Coates
MARK, *a young man of unknown parentage*	Richard Lewis
JENIFER, *his betrothed, a young girl*	Joan Sutherland
KING FISHER, *Jenifer's father, a business man*	Otakar Kraus
BELLA, *King Fisher's secretary*	Adele Leigh
JACK, *Bella's boy-friend, a mechanic*	John Lanigan
A VOICE	Monica Sinclair
A GIRL DANCER	Julia Farron
HALF-TIPSY MAN	Gordon Farrall
A MAN DANCING	Andrew Daniels
SOSOSTRIS, *a clairvoyante*	Oralia Dominguez
CHORUS *of Mark's and Jenifer's friends*	
DANCERS *attendant on the Ancients*	

Conductor: John Pritchard
Producer: Christopher West
Scenery and costumes by Barbara Hepworth
Choreography by John Cranko

4
Freedom of Choice
King Priam

After the production of *The Midsummer Marriage*, Tippett's first reaction was a feeling of intense relief that at long last the seven-year process of gestation was over, coupled with a strong disinclination to contemplate writing another opera in the near future; but this mood did not last long. In August 1957 he wrote to me saying:

I've had an unexpected commission from Koussevitzky Foundation, Washington, for a piece & at a high price. So I'm bucked by both the honour & the reward. I'm still negotiating about [what] it shall be. That is, I've only so far accepted & asked to be allowed to suggest. (They wanted a choral & orchestral piece of 20–30 minutes.)

On Webster's advice I saw Peter Brook & laid all my plans before him. . . . The exciting consequence is that a new opera is hardly to be avoided & at once, so to speak. The material is homeric & pre-homeric. Sounds mad – but you will see what it is. It isn't *Les Troyens* – that had nothing to do with it. And it is still much influenced by Brechtian methods, & the Milhaud–Claudel–Barrault production of *Christophe Colomb*. Epic theatre of course therefore. But no chiliastic philosophy, whether of a classless society or a heavenly reward. Shakespearean in temper. Tragic. . . .

The consultation with Peter Brook was helpful. The young producer considered Tippett's problem in the light of some of the criticisms that had been directed against the libretto of *The Midsummer Marriage* and gave him the following advice. 'Whatever subject you choose for your new opera,' he said, 'you are likely to choose a myth that has captured your imagination. But if you want your audience to follow you without difficulty, choose a public myth and not a private one.' This advice was taken to heart. On reflection Tippett found that the subject he wanted to tackle was itself connected with the problem of choice and that this could best be exemplified by taking a succession of episodes from the Trojan War, showing in particular how the exercise of moral choice affected the relations between King Priam and his second son Paris. Whereas *The Midsummer Marriage* had been basically a comedy, King Priam was conceived as a tragedy; and this implied a fundamental change of idiom.

The first thing the composer had to do was to get the Koussevitzky Foundation's commission transferred to the new opera; and this was successfully carried out by February 1958. During the following months he was busy finishing off *Crown of the Year*, the Badminton School Cantata; and in May he wrote to me saying: 'And behind it is boiling up the tragic story of Priam and his sons. Want you to see a scenario when I can get it finished. (I've been stealing time occasionally from *Crown* to do it!)'.

The raw material that he decided to use for his new opera – characters and action – was all to be found in the *Iliad*. Unlike the scenario of *The Midsummer Marriage*, there was no scope for fantasy or invention in *King Priam*, only a job of selection and presentation.

By the time the scenario reached me (December 1958), the greater part of the libretto was in draft. The composer had recognized the fact that this would be an epic drama ranging over various countries and through many years – a very different problem from *The Midsummer Marriage* with its unities of time and place and its lyrical expression of moods and emotions. Clearly a special stage technique was needed. Mindful of the example set by Brecht, Tippett planned the libretto of *King Priam* as a succession of short dramatic scenes connected by interludes in which some of the characters could provide narration and commentary like a chorus. The method was outlined in a stage direction at the end of the first scene where Priam has just given the order for his baby son Paris to be killed:

The Old Man and the Nurse come down to the footlights. By some easily manipulated change of dress, or by a mask perhaps, or a gesture, they can become a commenting Chorus. When speaking as Chorus they declaim; when speaking as expressive of their roles they do not declaim.

There are seven of these interludes in all; and they help the action to flow swiftly and smoothly between the scenes.

The opera also contains a cunning piece of compression. At a certain point in the story, Hermes appears to Paris as Messenger of Zeus, and this leads directly to the scene of the Judgement of Paris. Tippett decided that the three goddesses would be played by the three chief women in the cast, Hecuba, Andromache, and Helen. Not only was this an economical move, but it gave rise to an interesting nexus of implied relationships between the three goddesses and the three wives.

The scenario I read in December 1958 was very near a final draft. In a covering note (dated December 11) the composer wrote:

What we've been trying to do is to unify the theme and exclude as much of the mere story of the war as we reasonably can. Hermes, as Vermittler,* is an invention of Rennert's. In this latest version Patroclus has been suppressed altogether. I think for the better. He had no dramatic reality to this script. I've begun the music to Scene 1 because that is fairly agreed upon. I think Scene 2 also. . . .

But I thought he'd gone too far in cutting and suppressing material – one of the proposed deletions was the scene between Achilles and Patroclus in Achilles' tent – and I said so in a letter (dated December 14):

. . . I've just read the deleted scene in Achilles's tent, and I think it's excellent. It has nearly everything I want – a song for Achilles, a scene for Patroclus, a reference to Neoptolemus, a sight of the celebrated armour, and a mention of the great war cry. Without this scene and this preparation, the end of the act will fall quite flat. With it, you have an intensely dramatic curtain. . . .

The scenario I'd been shown was in two acts. I now strongly advocated a revised lay-out in three acts, which would mean that Act II would be a 'war' act for men's voices alone. The restitution of the scene in Achilles' tent and the redeployment of the dramatic material in three acts instead of two led almost directly to the final and definitive version of the opera libretto, which ran as follows:

ACT I SCENE I	Birth of Paris. Priam's meditation. 'A father and a king'.
INTERLUDE I	Choral commentary (Nurse, Old Man, Young Guard).
SCENE II	The bull hunt. Priam's monologue. 'So have I often hoped'.
INTERLUDE II	Choral commentary (Nurse, Old Man, Young Guard). Hector's wedding.
SCENE III	Paris and Helen. Appearance of Hermes. Paris's

*Go-between.

judgement of the three graces – Athene (Hecuba), Hera (Andromache), Aphrodite (Helen).

ACT II SCENE I	Hector and Paris with Priam. Hermes takes the Old
INTERLUDE I	Man through the Greek lines.
SCENE II	In Achilles's tent. Achilles and Patroclus.
INTERLUDE II	Hermes and the Old Man return to Troy.
SCENE III	The death of Patroclus. Thanksgiving by Hector, Priam and Paris. The war-cry of Achilles.
ACT III SCENE I	Andromache (alone); then Hecuba and Andromache; finally Helen, Hecuba and Andromache. Trio.
INTERLUDE I	Serving Women's commentary on Hector's death.
SCENE II	Priam and Paris, Young Guard, Old Man and Nurse.
INTERLUDE II	Instrumental.
SCENE III	In Achilles's tent. Achilles and Priam.
INTERLUDE III	Hermes, Messenger of Death.
SCENE IV	The death of Priam.

The composition of the music started in December 1958.

In the summer of 1959, Tippett received an enquiry from David Webster, who wanted to know whether he would allow the first performance of *King Priam* to be given in Coventry in May 1962 by the Covent Garden Opera Company as part of the Coventry Cathedral Festival. The reply was strongly in favour. Tippett had known Bishop Gorton and all his early plans and hopes for the rebuilding of the cathedral and had allowed some of his music to be used to accompany a British Council film, which had featured sequences showing Sir Basil Spence's model of the new cathedral and shots of John Hutton and his assistants at work on the clear engraved-glass panels of saints and angels in the great (south) window. He also thought that the theme of his opera, taken from an older war, would be 'tolerably appropriate' to the occasion. So it was agreed that the first performance of *King Priam* should be given at Coventry Theatre on 29 May 1962 with a London premiere a few days later. This was a reassuring move on the part of David Webster, especially if one recalled that *The Midsummer Marriage* had not won unanimous approval from the establishment at the Royal Opera House. 'No box office draw,' said Lord Drogheda sternly (then chairman of the Royal

Opera House, Covent Garden), referring to *Billy Budd* and *The Midsummer Marriage*; and in the case of the latter opera he added an admonitory rider about the composer who 'insists upon writing his own libretti; of doubtful literary quality but of quite undoubted obscurity'.*

When Tippett committed himself to the composition of *The Midsummer Marriage*, he had everything to learn about the technique of writing operas. By the time he came to tackle *King Priam* he seemed to have acquired a full professional mastery of the medium.

King Priam was conceived as a tragedy with a remote historical setting. This postulated a very different idiom from that of *The Midsummer Marriage* with its rich harmonic lyricism. The music in *King Priam* is stark, strong and bony. Thirds and sixths are, for the most part, conspicuous by their rarity, while there is a plethora of seconds, sevenths and ninths, and much of the harmonic structure is closely geared to chords featuring fourths and fifths.

Even before the rise of the curtain, the orchestra starts to create an atmosphere of violence. Trumpets and timpani in the orchestra pit and on the stage sketch the battleground in depth. Cries are heard from the chorus off-stage. Out of the confused calls of voices and instruments rises what seems like a series of scaling ladders of sound (trumpets). The music approaches a climax; the curtain rises; on the stage a point of light picks out a cradle; the orchestra is silent, apart from an oboe solo to speak for the new-born babe. A nurse comes on the stage, followed by Hecuba; a few bars later King Priam enters. The opera is launched.

Priam is the hero of the opera. Husband, father and king – it seemed necessary to cast him as a bass baritone; and the opera had to be written so that, as in *Boris Godunov*, his voice could penetrate or rise above the surrounding texture and dominate the musical scene. The interpretation of Hecuba's dream leads to the point where Priam realises that, if he is to avoid the fate of being killed by his own son, he must kill the child at once. To a low string accompaniment in thick five-part harmony, he sings:

A Father and a King.
O child who cannot choose to live or die, I
choose for you. The Queen is right. Let the child
be killed.

*Lord Drogheda, *Double Harness: Memories* (Weidenfeld & Nicolson, 1978).

He hands the child over to a young guard for the sentence to be carried out. But, in the event, the Young Guard allows his natural compassion to get the better of him, and Paris survives.

Twelve years or so later, Priam, his elder son Hector, and a few Huntsmen are in the country chasing bulls. Hector's skill excites the admiration of Priam and the Huntsmen. But suddenly 'a beautiful boy, younger than Hector' appears, sprung from nowhere, leaps on to the back of a bull and dashes off. Presently he returns, and his arrival on the scene is greeted by the orchestra with repeated rich string chords, the first of which is laced with an effervescent harp glissando which produces an effect of numinous radiance. A dialogue between Hector and the boy ensues – a passage of lightly accompanied recitative. The tone is a trifle naive.

BOY: Who are you then?
HECTOR: I am from Troy.
BOY: Are you a young hero?
HECTOR: O yes.
BOY: And I shall be a hero too.
    Can I go back with you to Troy?
    etc.

In the theatre the audience is surprised by the sudden arrival of a fresh unbroken voice (boy soprano). As soon as Priam returns to the stage, he is startled to find the boy in converse with Hector and asks him his name. 'Paris' is the reply.

The shock is so great that time seems to stand still; and the orchestra recalls a strange little fate motif first heard in Act I scene i, when a similar shock resulted from the Old Man's revelation that Paris was destined to kill his father.

Some of the music in Acts II and III features a strong heavy piano line, emphasized by octaves, double octaves, and even treble octaves, forming a kind of massive skeletal frame. These memorable, compelling motifs are not specifically associated with Priam himself, but seem to embody the essential idiom of the opera and to have haunted the composer's mind for several years after the completion of *King Priam*. Hence the appearance of some of this material almost unchanged in the second Piano Sonata (1962) and the Concerto for Orchestra (1963).

The last scene of the first act introduces a nubile Paris with tenor voice. He has a series of passionate exchanges with Helen, urging her to choose between her husband (Menelaus) and himself. She leaves the stage, but as he begins to realize the force of the love she has awakened in him, he wonders whether there's any free choice at all as far as he's concerned. At this point Hermes appears in his role as divine go-between with a message to Paris from Zeus, telling him he is to choose the most beautiful of the three goddesses – Athene, Hera, and Aphrodite. These parts are sung by Hecuba, Andromache, and Helen. The sound of strings is particularly closely associated with the first two – a vertiginously fast theme for unison violins with Hecuba, and a more expressive theme for unison cellos with Andromache. Helen does no more than murmur Paris's name softly and gently; the die is cast. Paris awards the apple to Aphrodite and is promptly cursed by Athene and Hera. He rushes out as the goddesses disappear. And from an empty stage Hermes issues his summons 'To Troy!'

The 'war' act follows (Act II), with no women (no strings) and the presence of two Greek warriors, Achilles and Patroclus, in the middle scene. Here we concentrate not on their involvement in the war, but on their personal passion.

The first scene – upon or beside the walls of Troy – reveals the extent of the bickering that has flared up between Hector (the hero) and Paris (the womanizer). 'I wish you were not so like a living hammer,' says Paris, adding, 'You tire me.' Priam tries to rally them. Hector in armour strides off to war. A little later Paris, now also in armour, follows him. The first interlude of this act crosses the battlefield, from the Trojan walls to the Greek lines; the second covers the return journey.

Scene ii shows Achilles in his tent in the Greek lines with his friend Patroclus. After the distant cries of 'War!' and scattered calls of trumpets and timpani, the orchestra is suddenly silent, and a new sound is heard – Achilles (heroic tenor) singing a strophic song to a lyre (guitar). This is the only lyrical moment in the opera, and it comes at the climactic halfway point. Although the song is written in two stanzas, it can be seen from the first line – 'O rich-soiled land of Phthia' – that there is nothing conventional about its literary style. The vocal line is highly ornamented, and the guitar is treated as a virtuoso instrument. The song moves Patroclus to tears. When it is over, he warns Achilles that his refusal to fight may lead to the defeat of the Greeks and asks if he will allow him (Patroclus) to disguise himself in Achilles' armour and attempt to drive the Trojans back across the plain. Achilles replies – 'Patroclus, you shall! The scheme is worthy of my fertile brain.' He looks out of the tent for a moment and exclaims, 'Hector has fired the ships. We act in the nick of time' – adding, 'More than my armour I'll lend you strength shouting my war-cry when the moment comes.' They pour a libation to Zeus, and Patroclus rushes out of the tent.

Like the first scene of Act II, the third scene is on or beside the walls of Troy. Hermes reports that 'a hero in Achilles' armour, perhaps Patroclus, has rushed headlong from the ships, driving all before him'. The Trojans rally; and news comes that Hector has killed Patroclus, stripped the body and put on Achilles' armour. Hector appears resplendent on the walls of Troy, and on his suggestion Priam and Paris join him in a trio of thanksgiving to Zeus, and (for good measure) to Apollo as well. The rhetoric of the occasion is such that the accompanying woodwind chords burst out into trills in all their parts. At the height of the ensemble, Achilles appears before the tent to deliver his war-cry, 'oi, – o, – o,o, oi, oi, oi, – oi, – o, – o, oi, oi, oi, – oi, – o', a blood-curdling melisma that echoes around the stage and calls for amplification if it is to make its full effect. He doesn't realize that it comes too late. The trio stops dead. Hector is transfixed by the cry; but the Old Man, who is lingering in the background, starts to gloat over the nude body of Patroclus where it lies outside the walls of Troy in no-man's-land. When Achilles delivers his cry a second time, parts of it modulate a tone higher; and when he delivers it a third time, it is screwed up still higher, nearly to breaking point. At this point the score calls for a quick curtain with absolute silence on the strong beat of the bar after Achilles, chorus and orchestra have been cut off dead at the end of his third war-cry.

In Act III the womenfolk reappear, so the orchestra returns to its normal disposition. The first scene starts with a solo for Andromache, awaiting Hector's return from fighting. Hecuba enters: the scene broadens to a bickering duet. Then Helen enters and is forthwith attacked by Andromache. She has an air in which she recalls how once, as she came along the walls of Troy, the old men spoke of her and said, 'No wonder Greeks and Trojans go to war for such a woman,' and she considered they spoke well, for she remembered she was Zeus' daughter, 'conceived when the great wings beat above Leda'.

This is the cue for a large-scale trio sung by the three women, in which they pray to those who have been their tutelary goddesses since the scene of the Judgement of Paris – Athene, Hera, and Aphrodite – and ask that balm of comfort be granted to their menfolk. Each of them knows that death is drawing near. At the end of the ensemble there is a passage accompanied only by six solo violins, three of them playing pizzicato and three *col legno*, where a Serving Woman says 'The bath is hot. Will the Lord Hector come?' and Andromache answers 'Yes, Yes, Yes' and goes. The remaining Serving Women come downstage as a chorus and answer 'No, No, No.' They know better – they always know. At this point, unexpectedly, the anonymity of the classical chorus begins to break down:

We always know
Yet who are we?
Not the names that figure in the drama.
Un-named. Slaves. (Yes.) Slaves.
To whom the fate of towered Troy is but a change of masters.

But there is no time to pursue this dialectical line, for Hector is dead, and someone must break the news to the king.

That person is Paris. And from Paris' first words Priam suspects the bad news concerns his eldest son, Hector. But he finds Paris' words, 'Achilles has killed him and shamefully misused him,' impossible to take in at a first hearing. 'Say that again,' he groans, and Paris repeats the deadly words, accompanied by the same quiet roll on the timpani as before. In his anguish he upbraids Paris. 'Why did *you* not kill Patroclus? Why did not *you* fight Achilles? O, I could have spared you well for Hector.' Goaded by his father's accusations of cowardice, Paris rushes off to kill Achilles.

In the latter part of this scene Priam talks to the Young Guard and the Old Man and rehearses the fatal chain of vengeance:

– Who killed Patroclus?
– Great Hector, defending the city.
– Who avenged Patroclus, killing Hector?
– Barbaric Achilles. Curse him!
– Who kills Achilles?
– Paris, my son.
– Who will kill Paris?
– Agamemnon.

At this point the Young Guard asks Priam if this is the vengeance that he wants and Priam replies, 'I do not want these deaths. I want my own.' This is sung to the same close-textured low string accompaniment in five-part harmony that was first heard in Act I Scene i when after the birth of Paris, Priam exclaimed, 'A father and a king.' In his anguish he now utters a general curse and specifically curses his soul that will not let him rest. He sinks to the ground in despair; and at the end of the scene the Nurse sings, 'Measure him time with mercy.'

Here comes a significant stage direction:

The time is measured by an instrumental interlude. The figures of Priam and the Chorus fade away, and only darkness is left, and moving shadows. When enough time is measured by the music, a point of light grows on the stage. It is Achilles at night in his tent (Scene iii). The corpse of Hector is covered by a cloth. Achilles sits brooding over the body.

A solo guitar is heard, as at the beginning of Act II Scene ii. Suddenly Priam enters, and Achilles starts up. Priam tries to reassure Achilles that he is unarmed and has come to ransom the body of his son; and as he says this, he glances at the cloth covering the corpse 'as though unable to control his trembling need to touch it'. At first Achilles is almost truculent. 'Were you not a father, old as my own father, I would kill you now.' He softens a little. 'There is indeed the body of Hector. But cruel though I am, I will not force you to uncover it. It is mutilated shamefully, and by my own hands.' Then he begins to break down.

> For this flesh is Hector's, and not –
> And not – and never –
> The living flesh of him I loved –
> The gentle prince, Patroclus.

And in his anguish he sits down, sobbing.

With a swift movement, Priam kneels before him, clasps his knees and kisses what he calls his 'terrible man-slaying hands'. Achilles is touched and feels pity for the old man, who he promises shall have the body of his son to take back to Troy. Then Achilles stands up to pray and addresses Patroclus in far-off Hades, begging him not to be angry when he hears that his lover has given Priam Hector's body back, but assuring him that he shall have his 'proper share of the princely ransom' that will be demanded. This short intensely moving scene is accompanied by two trumpets – one in the orchestral pit, and one behind the scenes, treated like an echo.

The scene ends with Priam and Achilles, sitting at a table, drinking wine and rehearsing their litany of deaths. 'I shall die first', says Achilles, 'and in battle. Which of the Trojans will kill me?' 'Paris,' says Priam, 'Paris, my son.' 'And who will kill you at the altar, King Priam?' asks Achilles. 'My goddess-mother told *me*, so I will tell *you*. Neoptolemus will kill you at the altar. Neoptolemus, *my* son.'

The greater part of the last interlude is devoted to a lyrical air for Hermes, 'O divine music', with piano and harp accompaniment and an *obligato* part for flute. This is a self-contained work; in 1963 the composer made a special wordless arrangement of it for flute, oboe, and piano (or harpsichord) under the title *Prelude, Recitative and Aria*.

The last scene features Priam before an altar in Troy. The Greeks have broken into the city; and there is a continuous noise of battle. Paris arrives with the news that he has killed Achilles. But Priam is not interested. Paris suggests that he should take Helen and Priam to found another Troy elsewhere, to be answered by Priam with the astute remark: 'You are not the founding sort.'

Hecuba arrives; but Priam refuses to see her. It is the same with Andromache. But when Helen arrives, Priam agrees to speak to her.

Meanwhile the trumpets and drums and cries from the Prelude to Act I have returned with increasing urgency, and also the scaling ladders of sound. The city has started to burn. At the end of a short dialogue, Priam kisses Helen, who goes. He sinks down before the altar and tries to speak, but cannot be heard above the din. Hermes appears as a god; there is a sudden respite in the noise of battle, and Priam can just be heard trying to say something that harks back to the mood of Hermes's air in the last interlude:

I see mirrors
Myriad upon myriad moving
The dark forms
Of creation.

After Hermes has descended to Hades, Neoptolemus bursts on to the stage with a party of Greeks and runs his sword through Priam at the altar, who dies instantly. There is nothing left over in the drama and music except silence – and a few bars of inward tears like the ghost of the theme that occurred earlier on when time stood still for a moment.

Work on the composition of the opera proceeded smoothly. The three-act score took nearly three years to complete and was ready by the end of 1961. Arrangements for the production at Covent Garden proceeded equally smoothly. Sam Wanamaker was appointed producer, and Sean Kenny designer. These were both excellent choices and the production won universal commendation. John Pritchard conducted; and Forbes Robinson scored a great personal success in the title role. Nearly all the music critics were enthusiastic. Whereas after the premiere of *The Midsummer Marriage* the newspapers had featured such headlines as, 'This Opera Baffles Us Too, Say Singers', 'Opera Marred By Obscurity', 'Nonsense, but it's Music', the press now agreed that *King Priam* revealed Tippett as 'a Master of Opera'. The opera was revived for the 1962–3 and 1966–7 seasons at Covent Garden and the first German production was given at the Badisches Staattheater, Karlsruhe, on 26 January 1963 in a German translation by Walter Bergmann. The musical direction was in the hands of Arthur Grüber.

Even so it was extraordinary to find there were still people not prepared to accept Tippett's mastery in instrumentation and who contended that some passages in the score were unplayable. For instance, it was thought that the strings could not do justice to Hecuba's running passages for unison violins, so these were curtailed in favour of the piano as an alternative instrument. Perhaps in the course of time these and other unnecessary changes will be completely eradicated from the material for performance.

The pencil manuscript of the full score was handed over to the Koussevitzky Music Foundation to fulfil one of the conditions of the original commission and is to be found in the Library of Congress, Washington DC. The ink manuscript is in the British Library.

KING PRIAM

First performed 29 May 1962
Coventry Theatre, Coventry
(as part of the Coventry Festival)

Opera in three acts.
Words and Music by Michael Tippett

NURSE	Noreen Berry
HECUBA, *Priam's wife*	Marie Collier
PRIAM, *King of Troy*	Forbes Robinson
OLD MAN	David Kelly
YOUNG GUARD	Robert Bowman
HECTOR, *eldest son of Priam and Hecuba*	Victor Godfrey
PARIS (*as a young boy*), *Priam's second son*	Philip Doghan
PARIS (*as a man*)	John Dobson
HELEN, *wife to Menelaus of Sparta, then wife in adultery to Paris*	Margreta Elkins
HERMES, *messenger of the Gods*	John Lanigan
ANDROMACHE, *Hector's wife*	Josephine Veasey
ACHILLES, *a Greek hero*	Richard Lewis
PATROCLUS, *his friend*	Joseph Ward
SERVING WOMAN	Paula Dean
HUNTERS, WEDDING GUESTS, SERVING WOMEN, etc.	

Conductor: John Pritchard
Producer: Sam Wanamaker
Scenery and costumes by Sean Kenny
Lighting by William Bundy

5
Seven Men and Women
of Our Time
The Knot Garden

For his next opera, Tippett reverted to the contemporary scene of the 1950s and 1960s and decided to construct another of his private mythologies. In the introduction to *Moving into Aquarius*, he had referred to his central preoccupation with the question of 'what sort of world we live in and how we may behave in it'. This pointed to the direction the new opera was to take.

The libretto was under intensive discussion from early 1963 to about the end of 1965. His starting-point was his wish to present a number of different contemporary characters, all of whom were to be of more or less equal operatic importance. There would be no leading man or woman, and no chorus. The action would explore the characters' relationships with each other, particularly as set off by the presence of a psychoanalyst. Among them would be a husband and wife, whose marriage was in danger of break-up. The wife would be the hostess and would spend a lot of time in her garden. The remaining characters would be guests.

The idea of a garden setting turned out to be central to the opera. It so happened that Tippett's house at Corsham had a particularly fine enclosed garden on the edge of the park; and his most recent big-scale composition had been *The Vision of St Augustine* in which Augustine and his mother stand together at a window in Ostia looking into an inner garden (*hortus conclusus*). But neither of these gardens seems to have served as model for the opera. In an early letter postmarked 27 February 1963 he wrote to me:

The renaissance rose garden had always (it appeared) lovers, a fountain, and music. (The negro with a guitar?) Allied, I should say, to the Shakespearean idea of 'music' counter-poised to 'tempest' – or the sea in destructive action. ... So the 'music', in this sense, forms as the garden forms – and as the lovers, or lover, speaks. The whole charade could be Persian or Indian or Italian. But it'll depend finally on what the characters (in charade) force on us.

A little later he continued his meditations in another letter.

The garden may indeed be Persian; but I suspect the psychiatrist dreams of himself as the gardener! Especially if the garden, as it is, is 'possessed' by a woman. So you might open a T opera for once in full sunlight, with the psychiatrist and secateurs trimming the roses. But she is somewhere in the garden too, of course. . . .

As background to the idea of the charade, he had in mind the extraordinary effect of Edward Albee's play *Who's Afraid of Virginia Woolf?* where with only two pairs of lovers on the stage, the playwright allowed the elder married couple to play a succession of games in which they tried out the possibilities of different emotional patternings – an intensive play therapy that was to lead to an ultimate Shakespearean mood of forgiveness.* Already the setting and characters were beginning to form and Shakespeare's *Tempest* was at hand to provide a cue for the charade.

The concept of the garden implied the presence of a house nearby, and of a workaday world outside the enclosing wall. There might be a fountain in the garden, and at times the garden paths might remind one of a maze. By August 1964 the composer was suggesting the following possible titles for his new opera: *The Garden*; *Charade*; *The Maze Garden*; *The Amazing Garden*. A little later he fixed on *The Knot Garden*.

It was time now to choose the characters. To begin with, it was decided there should be eight in all, four men and four women. It was important that at an early stage they should be named, for without names they seemed unable to come to life, and it was difficult to talk about nameless persons, to try to develop their characters, and speculate on how they might behave in certain circumstances. The psychiatrist was to be called Mangus. The hostess/gardener was to be Thea, with the name's deliberate suggestion of an earth-goddess. Her husband, a civil engineer, was Faber. The Latin connotations of the word seemed to please the composer, with their meanings of 'maker' and 'worker', and perhaps he liked also to be reminded of the publishing house where his friend, T. S. Eliot, had worked for many

---

*cf. *Love in Opera IV*, a set of unscripted talks on opera which Tippett made for the Canadian Broadcasting Corporation in 1969, and later redrafted for publication.

years and which had published most of his books. Faber and Thea were to have a young girl, their ward, staying with them, and her presence was to complicate the marital set-up. It seemed appropriate for her to be called Flora. Thea was to have a younger sister, a dedicated freedom fighter, who had taken part in the Resistance movement and been captured and tortured. The example of the French Resistance seemed to demand a partly French name, and Denise was chosen. Then there were to be a couple of 'gay' friends: a white musician in his thirties, and a negro writer in his late twenties. Quite early on Tippett decided the negro should be called Mel – a taste of honey (*miel*). At first his musician friend was called Piers, but at a later stage this was changed to Dov. The eighth and last character was Claire, a hospital doctor rising forty.

These eight characters formed a somewhat volatile and potentially explosive mixture. Although there were four men and four women, there was a degree of imbalance in their relationship, though not necessarily because Dov and Mel were homosexual. (In fact, they seemed to be bisexual rather than homosexual.) Mangus seemed to stand both outside and inside the action – an analyst, a magician, a kind of Prospero figure.

By August 1964 Tippett knew the opera would be divided into three acts and subtitled them: Act I, Confrontation; Act II, Labyrinth; Act III, Charade. At this time he wrote me a letter about the way he thought the action would develop, saying:

So far as I've got, Act I sets out the characters as quickly and simply as possible, with hints of the inner values of each which make relationship difficult e.g. Faber's engineering, Thea's 'mysticism', Claire's surgical asceticism, Mel's race, Dov's music and so on. But these things are shown as only potentially explosive within some pattern of manners. The Catalyst is Denise who brings the 'outside' in with denunciatory violence, which provokes Mel to the blues that ends the act.

In Act II the maze begins to operate and in a series of meetings and departures nearly every 'coupling' is 'broken up' – though only that of Mel and Dov finally – so that when Flora and Dov are thrown clear (downstage) of the whirling maze at the end, it's Dov's heartbreak that, though comforting the frightened Flora, starts him singing the music that makes the garden flower for a moment. When the music stops, the 'reality' returns. This is dangerously near to sentimentality, but maybe can be managed. Even Mel's 'Come I taught you that!'

In Act III we need some surrealist goings-on (with Mangus trying to play Prospero?) or some ritual that takes the action deeper into some moment of truth, or better some absurdity which gets the characters into some take-it-or-leave-it existentialist ground. (This is what I mean by dadaist tradition). This means, I think, that the Spring or Fountain is highly meta-phoricised, even into some horse-play of Mangus, and the music must be equally 'dadaist' or 'absurd', where the ridiculous meets the sublime. From this point everything and everybody unwinds until Faber and Thea are alone and together for the first time and must speak directly as man and wife – which is the curtain.

When in April 1965 the composer came to draft his first synopsis, which he entitled *A Touch of Caliban*, he found he was becoming clearer about a number of technical points. For instance, in *King Priam* the scenes within the various acts had been joined by inter-ludes, during which different groups of characters assumed the functions of a chorus commenting on the action while the scene changes went on behind a drop curtain. But in *The Knot Garden* the composer wished to use a form of 'dissolve' or 'black-out', which would enable each act to move through 'a swift series of sharply delineated short scenes' (in the French dramatic sense) and would 'culminate in, or be swept away by, essentially musical forms of con-siderable length (in proportion to the preparatory scenes)'.

From this style of presentation he deduced there was no point in adhering to naturalistic or realistic stage conventions and decided the piece would gain, not lose, in force and impact, if all attempted rational explanations were dispensed with and more emphasis placed on the surreal elements of the characters. He felt that the interplay of the real and the surreal, of the outer and inner relationships, was continually involving threesomes as well as twosomes. In this synopsis (*A Touch of Caliban*) there was a scene near the end of Act II where after Dov/Ariel was granted his liberty, Mel floored him and while Mel was being dragged off, Dov lay prostrate, waving his legs in the air and crying, 'I want to be raped!' Tippett's comment, in the intro-duction to the synopsis, was

The melodramatic shock sentence Dov uses is as much about the possibility that our 'white' society is in an unconscious masochistic relation towards the 'black' – or the 'middle' class towards the 'working' class etc. – as about the sado-masochistic bases of some human relationships.

The fact that in the final draft of the libretto this particular line was cut does not really alter the fact that in his work Tippett has always been deeply concerned with the collective as well as the individual condition of mankind.

It will be noticed that in the draft synopsis, *A Touch of Caliban*, he planned each act to end with 'essentially musical forms of considerable length'.

In Act I the last of the characters to arrive in the knot garden is Denise. Just as she dominates the stage with her 'half-majestic, half-sinister' appearance (for the stage direction in the libretto tells us 'she is twisted and otherwise disfigured from the effects of torture'), so her aria 'O, you may stare in horror' dominates in sustained intensity and horror the music of the rest of the act. This is a great operatic number by any standards, and only a big finale, an ensemble for all the other characters who have listened to Denise's frightening analysis of pain and denunciation of torture, could bring the act to a successful conclusion. This is the Blues ensemble, a sextet led by Mel, 'Do, do not, do not torment me'.

Act II was not easy to fix. It was to open with the garden in disarray and the maze in operation – in short successive scenes a couple would draw in a third person and eject one of the original two. This shuffling process was to go at allegro speed and give the effect of spiralling variations. At one point the composer thought the finale of this act might be 'the hint of an endless repetition, but spinning faster and faster, with possibly a sudden stop and tableau before the curtain comes down'. On the other hand he realized that a different ending whereby the music turned away from the obvious *da capo* repetition to some 'loop' out of the endless recurrence would be exciting if this 'loop' were the right one; and he wondered if the two lost 'children', Flora and Dov, might be thrown out of the whirling maze or pushed out by Mangus, and meet on a calm forestage. He wrote: 'Out of his heartbreak and the need to comfort Flora, Dov at last produces a hint of the music to which the rose-garden can appeal.' Another alternative was an ending which would disclose Mangus 'at work' as it were. In the end it was the Flora/Dov ending that won the day and it was the inspired choice of a fragment of Schubert recollected in this sudden tranquillity that unlocked the door to a different song, a lyric sung by Dov, which ended, 'O honey, honey, make love to me . . . in the fabulous rose-garden.' This was to have even wider implications than its operatic setting, for when *The Knot Garden* was finished, Tippett took this song and made it the first of a cycle of three independent *Songs for Dov* for tenor and orchestra.

The third act caused more difficulty than either of the other two. It was to open with various charade scenes from *The Tempest* played by Mangus as Prospero, Flora as Miranda, Faber as Ferdinand, Dov as Ariel, and Mel as Caliban, and the non-playing characters as audience. As the synopsis made clear, only the chess game is a scene originally enacted by Shakespeare's characters. Some of the other scenes are merely described by Shakespeare, but not played. And the final scene – what is the future of Ariel and Caliban to be? – is invented. Then comes what the composer calls a stage free-for-all, representing the furthest point of release, which issues in an ensemble of irony. This breaks through the various conventions that have been established – *The Tempest*, the island, the garden, the maze, and even the special relationship between the actors on the stage and the audience in the theatre.

This is the moment when Mangus/Prospero breaks his staff and drowns his book (metaphorically, if not actually), and the guests take their leave and depart, leaving Faber and Thea alone on the stage for the first time in the course of the opera. Night has fallen, and here Tippett was irresistibly reminded of the end of Virginia Woolf's last novel, *Between the Acts*. As he quoted it in his draft synopsis, the passage runs as follows:

Left alone together for the first time that day, they were silent. Alone, enmity was bared; also love. Before they slept, they must fight; after they had fought, they would embrace. From that embrace another life might be born. But first they must fight, as the dog-fox fights with the vixen, in the heart of darkness, in the fields of night. . . . It was night. . . . It was night before roads were made, or houses. It was the night that dwellers in caves had watched from some high place among rocks. Then the curtain rose. They spoke.

At this stage the composer was uncertain whether the scene could be mimed with the words whispered into a microphone, or whether some paraphrase of the scene could be played direct.

By the end of October 1965, he was revising the Epilogue, and on the 27th he wrote to my wife saying:

I came entirely to your view that the epilogue can't be Woolf. So last night I hammered away at it in Blake–Whitman–Lawrence aphorisms. It very nearly works. But the second pair of separate lines is still the crux. I see Thea and Faber standing up from their seats, but can't quite hammer that gesture into the thought in the way the seed-packets and the factory papers encompass garden and works. The thought isn't quite concrete in the right way. And maybe it's the notion of enmity (in the Woolf) which has got elided. And writing out that sentence to you nearly gave it me, *i.e.* when they stand up they are certainly themselves entire but still unable to 'imagine' the other (in Blake's sense)*. I'll get it quite soon.

And he did! He got it as soon as he'd put the letter into its envelope and sealed it down, for on the outside of the envelope flap he scribbled – *Now I stand up – Faber: man: maker: myself.* And something to match for Thea.' And that was the solution.

Shortly before this correspondence about the Epilogue took place, there had been a major change in the opera. When the libretto was first circulated in draft, some of the persons it was shown to came to the conclusion that all the characters were pulling their weight with one exception – Claire. The more one scrutinized the action, the clearer it became that she was a minor character, and as *The Knot Garden* was designed to be an opera with no minor characters, she was obviously expendable. So it was decided she should be removed. The opera immediately gained in concision and density. The remaining seven characters succeeded in taking up the slack caused by her disappearance, and in various ways seven proved a better number to cater for than eight. Perhaps the loss of a woman in the team helped to emphasize the feminine traits in the Dov/Mel partnership. Another consequence of her disappearance was to reduce the size of the audience for the charades from *The Tempest*.

By the end of October 1965 the composer was writing: 'I expect I shall have to let the music start soon. But as that is always very slow in accumulating, the constant reconsideration of the details in the later part of the text can go on.' In fact, this reconsideration didn't go on for much longer. By 1966 he had started to compose the music, and composition proceeded roughly at the rate of an act a year, so that the opera was finished by the spring of 1969, its first performance being given at the Royal Opera House on 2 December 1970.

---

*In his letter Tippett enclosed this draft of the epilogue:
THEA: I put away the seed-packets.
FABER: I put away the factory papers.
BOTH: I encompass the vast night with an image of desire.
FABER: I stand up as myself to reach Thea's body in my vision.
THEA: I stand up as myself, for Faber now knows I am present.
BOTH: The war between us is transcended in desire.
THEA: Memory recedes in the moment.
FABER: I am all imagination.
[*They are about to move towards each other*].
BOTH: The curtain rises.

When he was working on libretto and score, he roughly calculated that the running time would total 127 minutes, made up as follows: Act I, 45 minutes; Act II, 36 minutes; Act III, 46 minutes. When the opera came to performance, it was discovered, to everyone's surprise including that of the composer, that the running time (without intervals) was only 87 minutes, made up as follows: Act I, 31; Act II, 23; Act III, 33. There's no doubt that Tippett's new 'dissolve' technique contributed substantially to making this score concentrated and succinct, particularly when compared with the leisurely progress of *The Midsummer Marriage*. In *The Knot Garden* he showed himself capable of a concentration of expression that reminded one of the final act of Berg's *Wozzeck* and some of Stravinsky's later serial works.

The first act opens with a kind of prologue – Mangus lying on a couch as a still point in a whirling storm. The orchestra presents a twelve-note theme with many unison or octave couplings, which gives the momentary illusion that the music may be about to exploit the serial technique, but this is by no means the case. The chromatic storm subsides, and Mangus rises from his couch, which disappears. A pulsing repeated chord from an electric guitar (the instrument's first appearance in one of Tippett's opera scores) leads directly to the 'dissolve' music marked *brillante* and *martellato*. The clatter of consecutive descending piano sevenths, topped with shrill piccolo, flute and violin triplets ends with a timpani drum-roll that leads back into the garden. Above a rich mulch of sound from the horns, Thea sings a tough and spiky arioso about planting and pruning, which is interrupted by Flora's whimpering screams (off). Flora rushes on to the stage, and Faber follows hard on her heels. This is the cue for a hard and bitter duet between wife and husband. Thea upbraids Faber: 'you should father her, not play the lecher'. 'A mother bitch!' is Faber's exasperated comment. Then he remembers something; his voice falls – 'And yet my wife;' and he goes off to the factory. Left alone on the stage, Mangus soliloquizes and recalls the following words of Prospero's in *The Tempest* – spoken just before the first appearance of Ariel:

... and by my prescience
I find my zenith doth depend upon
A most auspicious star ...

This is the cue for another 'dissolve'.

Thea and Flora have come from the inner garden. Thea sings, 'You can pick roses, arrange them in a bowl.' Flora is distracted and hums the tune of 'Eeny, meeny, miny, moe'. Suddenly she remembers a message she had forgotten to give Thea from her sister, Denise. 'She comes here – today – later.' Thea leaves the stage, and Flora goes on humming.

Presently a noisy hullabaloo, including the sounds of electric guitar and jazz-kit, announces the arrival of Dov and Mel – Dov dressed as Ariel and Mel as Caliban. They stop and remain so motion-less that Flora comes gingerly forward as if to touch them. Suddenly Dov speaks, with exaggeratedly broad vowels: 'If you think we're waxworks, you ought to pay, you know. Waxworks weren't made to be looked at for nothing. No how!' And Mel replying in a preter-naturally low voice says: 'Contrariwise, if you think we're alive, you ought to speak.' Involuntarily, Flora joins in the game with a tiny voice like a stage Alice. 'I'm sure I'm very sorry.' And then she bursts through this pretence and pleads: 'O, do stop play-acting; I'm real somewhere; I'm Flora.' And Dov and Mel, breaking up their pose, fall in: 'We're real too, somewhere' and explain that as they're acting a scene together – music by Dov, words by Mel – they've assumed the characters of Ariel and Caliban. The new ditty that they sing is:

Ca-ca-Caliban
Was a bad man
But Ariel was fairy
He could fly through the air
Invisible
But Caliban was scaly.

The bit of surrealist nonsense from *Alice in Wonderland* is an excellent approach to a series of scenes, or non-scenes, as soon as the ditty sung by Dov and Mel is over, starting with Thea's entrance carrying a tray of cocktails (homage to T. S. Eliot?). Mangus, Dov, Mel and Flora are on the stage. The orchestra repeats an icy cold series of chords (*Lento*) for glockenspiel alternating with xylophone; and after four bars of this, there is a chilly silence, broken by Thea's comment, 'Children at play.' The procession of glockenspiel/xylo-phone chords is resumed as Thea puts the cocktail tray down on the table. There is no chance for her to make another remark, for Mangus now takes up the commentary.

Adults too play later:
Plays within the play.
Ariel, Caliban, Ferdinand, Miranda:
All shall appear when I play Prospero.

Mangus and Flora go off together to get costumes for the charade, leaving Thea, Dov and Mel behind. Once again the icy cocktail glockenspiel/xylophone chords recur, as (to use the wording of the stage direction)

The triangle-trio that is left survey each other as in a ritual dance. Each man takes a glass from Thea's tray and she takes one herself. They lift the glasses to drink. As they do so Mel is drawn away to Thea so that Dov is isolated. Thea like Circe draws Mel hypnotically, by implication sexually, into the garden.

Dov smashes his glass to smithereens and goes down on all-fours, howling like Ariel's dog, and this is the posture he is in when Faber suddenly returns from the office. Faber looks at him in some astonishment; but Dov braves it out by dancing round him, and repeating his Ca-ca-Caliban ditty. The following dialogue, with its fascinating innuendos, ensues:

FABER: Who in hell are you?
DOV: My name is Dov; a musician.
   For the moment as you see,
   I'm dressed as Ariel.
FABER: 'But Ariel was fairy'.
   Who then is Caliban?
DOV: My friend Mel is Caliban.
   (Or will be when we play the scene.)
FABER: A curious friend.
DOV: We share together.
   (Or did till now.)
FABER: I see. I see.
   Come closer: to me: Faber.

And at this point the cocktail music returns – but changed. It has lost its icy glockenspiel/xylophone tinkle, and the chords are now played in menacing fashion by deep brass bass, alternating with a single (non-repeated) chord played by woodwind, electric guitar, piano and strings. The stage direction states:

By implication sexually provocative, Faber whistles jauntily. Dov moves across the stage as though fascinated. But before they meet, and with a strange sobbing cry from the orchestra, Thea and Mel are there on the opposite side of the stage. The resultant tableau cannot become a vocal ensemble because the tensions are not ready for such expression.

Nothing is sung in these short non-vocal episodes. Most of the sexual and other emotions implicit in the silent confrontation of these characters are worked out later in the opera – particularly in the second act when the device of the whirling maze is put into operation. But meanwhile these short scenes remain some of the most original and provocative passages in contemporary opera. They say something complicated that can perhaps only be expressed in operatic terms.

The finale follows, with Flora acting as Denise's advance guard. Her aria, 'O you may stare in horror', is one of the ·few great art numbers to have come out of the bestial cruelties and tortures of our times. It is almost unbearably vivid and upsetting; and the only way to follow it was to plan a big ensemble of compassion. This was the Blues, 'Do, do not, do not torment me', led by Mel, joined by Dov, Flora, Faber, Thea, and shortly before the end by Mangus (as Prospero) and finally topped off by Denise's screams.

In Act II the sequence of interrupted duets starts with the two sisters, Thea and Denise, singing together. But this is no real duet, and they do not properly converse – they merely accept a common metrical framework. Thea is whirled off as Faber is whirled on: and now a fragment of true dialogue occurs. Denise sings, 'I do not know your needs: I hardly know my own,' just before being whirled off. When Flora is whirled on, she is found to be still as she was in Act I – a little girl lost, trying to choose between the flowers she's picked – 'Eeny, meeny, miny, moe'. Her confrontation with Faber is no more successful than were previous meetings and Faber becomes increasingly exasperated at her unwillingness to stand and deliver her flowers. Terrified, she starts whimpering, drops the flowers, and is whirled off as Thea is whirled on again. This scene marks the nadir of the relationship between husband and wife. Thea produces a horse-whip and strikes Faber with it, spitting at him:

> Without the divine Furies,
> Who are women,
> There'd be no retribution.

Faber tries to defend himself, but is forced to the ground. Thea is whirled off, and Dov whirled on. Dov finds it strange that Faber should be on all fours, and he makes an ironic comment by barking

('Bow-wow') and howling ('Ow, ow, ow'). His enquiry, 'Has some woman put you down?' elicits the answer, 'Ah! Dov: you should know – Has a woman never put you down?' 'No: no woman,' cries Dov; and there is a sudden return of the menacing orchestral chords that accompanied Faber's provocative invitation to Dov in Act I. The scene between the two men is now pushed further, and Faber uncovers the hint of a split between Dov and Mel. Dov protests, 'What are you at, Faber? Probing to mock?' And Faber, still in a jaunty and mocking mood, replies:

I'm curious.
I had to know
You ... Dov, what if I
Want you: have power
To tempt, to force? Come,
I never kissed a man before.

But he is whirled off before he can put the matter to the test, and Mel is whirled on.

The scene between Dov and Mel is prefaced by the hullabaloo music that accompanied Dov and Mel's entry in Act I when they were dressed as Ariel and Caliban. They now play it like a song-and-dance routine against a fast and bitter blues background with the refrain:

One day we meet together, brother,
One day we meet together, brother,
One day we move apart.

At the end of the number Dov is whirled off as Denise is whirled on.

The following scene is really a solo air for Denise accompanied in four-part harmony by strings, horn and one or two other instruments. Denise sings:

Words are weapons
In the fight
For freedom, justice, dignity.
Your race calls you;
Calls for your words,
For your strength, for your love.

And this seems to touch a deep and sensitive spot in Mel. As though he heard in his mind 'We Shall Overcome', words are forced from him – 'O deep in my heart.' His bass baritone voice inserts itself un-obtrusively into the four-part musical accompaniment to Denise's air and opens up his innermost feelings. The effect is extremely poignant and recalls the way in *A Child of Our Time* Tippett dealt with bridge-passages designed to serve a similar function by leading into the negro spirituals. At this point the maze appears suddenly to go into reverse and to accelerate. There is a chaotic coming and going of characters, of whom two – Dov and Flora – are ejected on to the fore-stage. This is followed by a 'dissolve' (the first in this act) which leaves Dov and Flora alone together, and Dov tries to comfort her. As he rocks her gently in his arms, she stops crying. He asks if she likes music – if she ever sings – and her answer is to sing two lines from a Schubert Lied, '*In grün will ich mich kleiden.*' The romantic Schubert idiom comes over like a refreshing draught of cool water at this particular moment. Tippett's music modulates into this Schubert quotation with consummate skill, and moves away from it with equal mastery, a brief variation with piano descant accompanying Dov as he picks up the song from Flora, and supplies an English translation. This magical touch of Schubert puts Tippett's own score into historical perspective and helps to add a dimension to the idiom of the opera. At the end of her snatch of Schubert, Flora sings:

> Sometimes I dream I am a boy,
> Who dies for love.
> And then I am a girl again.
> Dov, you understand.

And Dov responds gently:

> I understand.
> Yet you're a bud that hasn't opened.
> Let's sing a different song.

'And he stands up to sing his first song.'*

This three-verse song is crucial to the understanding of Dov as a character in the opera and to his subsequent development in *Songs for Dov*. In a programme note for the latter work Tippett referred to the mixture of musical metaphors in his libretto and stressed the ambivalence of the elaborate part for electric harpsichord or guitar. He wrote:

The timbre produced by the amplification draws our ear to jazz (using the term as a wide generality) and America, while the activity of the instru-

---

*This appears as a stage direction in the vocal score, but not in the libretto. It implies the arrival, at some later date, of other songs for Dov.

mentalist's fingers on the harpsichord or guitar (more obviously on the stage than in the concert hall) draws us to the European operatic tradition of the stage serenado. And of course, lovers listening to music in the enclosed garden is part of what might be called the syndrome of the traditional 'fabulous rose-garden'.

When the third verse comes, and Dov sings:

O hold our fleeting youth for ever.
O stop the world I want to get off –

there is a stage direction:

Under the influence of Dov's music the rose-garden begins to form. By the last verse of the song it is all there: the enclosing walls, the fountain, the girl, the lover. As the song ends, a shadow enters the garden. It is Mel. He taps the lover on the shoulder.

MEL: I taught you that.
DOV: It is false.

At that point the garden starts to fade; and there is a musical coda consisting of the slow unrolling, decrescendo, of a phrase consisting of all twelve notes of the chromatic scale, which turns out to be a non-serial gesture, like the storm opening of Act I, and is not followed up.

Act III is the 'charade' act. Mangus returns to the scene for the first time since Act I and acts as Prospero. In addition, four of the remaining characters in the opera have roles in the charade: Dov–Ariel, Mel–Caliban, Flora–Miranda, and Faber–Ferdinand. Thea and Denise remain themselves. Anyone may be a spectator when not playing a scene in the charade. As soon as the curtain rises, Mangus puts on his cloak and describes a circle with his wand. Both Denise and Thea step into Mangus's circle; and this precipitates the 'dissolve' music, which leads to the first scene of the charade. Mangus–Prospero and Flora–Miranda are exploring the island on their first day. Miranda is as old as in *The Tempest*. Mel–Caliban is crawling about dumb. Mangus–Prospero behaves like a circus master and persuades him to stand upright. 'How clever you are, father!' is Flora–Miranda's admiring comment. Meanwhile cries come from a neighbouring tree: 'Freedom: freedom. Air. Light.' It is Dov–Ariel shut in the tree; and Mangus–Prospero frees him with the help of his book. 'How kind you are, father!' is Flora–Miranda's admiring comment. 'Caliban and Ariel: mine to command,' comments Mangus–Prospero, 'theirs to be grateful.' At this point he splits open the tree. Dov–Ariel rushes out and flings himself on Mel–Caliban, shouting:

> Your filthy mother Sycorax is dead;
> But you're alive alright.
> I've waited centuries for this.

And he belabours Mel–Caliban. Mangus–Prospero tries to haul Dov–Ariel off his victim to Dov–Ariel's annoyance:

> DOV–ARIEL: Hands off: I do but play my part.
> MEL–CALIBAN: O no: you went beyond the script.
> DOV–ARIEL: As I shall always do.

And a moment later the scene ends with an ascending, rather than a descending 'dissolve'.

In the generally accepted sense of the word, which seems to have come into fashion about the time of Jane Austen's youth, 'charade' was understood to mean 'a kind of riddle, in which each syllable of a word to be guessed, and sometimes the word itself, was enigmatically described, or acted'. This is not the case here. The opening operatic charade scene is (quite simply) a surrealist parable about colonization.

After comment from the spectators, there is another 'dissolve' – this time a descending one – which leads to a scene of attempted rape (in mime). The stage direction runs:

Flora–Miranda is asleep. Dov–Ariel is on guard. Mangus–Prospero is watching through a telescope. Mel–Caliban creeps on and up to the sleeping girl. Mangus–Prospero signals to Dov–Ariel to be ready. Mel–Caliban suddenly leaps on Flora–Miranda: pinning her arms, he tries to tear the clothes off her. She wakes and screams. At the dramatic instant Denise appears and hauls Mel–Caliban off and to his feet. Flora–Miranda runs off.

After more comment from the spectators, some of it directed in a critical spirit against Mangus–Prospero, he hands his telescope to Thea with a dignified gesture:

> Take the glass yourself.
> Now by my art
> You shall savour such a scene
> Of tender reconciliation
> As dreams may show,
> Holding the mirror up to nature.
> Ariel: disclose.

This is the cue in Tippett's score for an abbreviated 'dissolve'. The following charade scene is based directly on a few lines from Act V of Shakespeare's play, where Prospero discovers Ferdinand and Miranda playing at chess:

MIRANDA: Sweet lord, you play me false,
                              No, my dear'st love,
FERDINAND: I would not for the world.

In the case of Tippett's charade, Dov–Ariel discloses Faber–Ferdinand and Flora–Miranda playing chess; and Tippett superimposes on Shakespeare's scene a surrealist interpretation that produces a very different result:

FLORA–MIRANDA: [*Quoting with exaggerated rhetoric: a caricature of false innocence*]
'Sweet lord you play me false!'
FABER–FERDINAND: [*Quoting with exaggerated rhetoric: a caricature of false charm*]
'No my dearest love,
I would not for the world.'
FLORA–MIRANDA: [*sending the chess-board flying*]
O yes you would.
False: false.
Dov–Ariel lend me your wings.
I'm free: I'm free.

She runs off. Faber–Ferdinand's comment is, 'That scene went wrong!' Mangus–Prospero's is, 'That scene went right!'

This leads to an important musical aria for Thea, when she is left alone on the stage after Flora–Miranda, Dov–Ariel, Mangus–Prospero and Faber–Ferdinand have gone off. The charade therapy is beginning to work on her in her role of impassioned spectator; and her opening *andante*:

I am no more afraid.
So we swing full-circle back
Towards the sanctuary of marriage.
O strange enigma!

is accompanied by light wispy *glissandi* from woodwind, harp and strings. Halfway through her aria the tempo changes to *meno mosso*, and as she recalls how,

> This morning my garden seemed a sanctuary
> From where I hated him and fought all day . . .
> I am no more afraid——

the horn music that accompanied her morning visit returns with its rich mulch of sound. The figuration of some of the semiquaver triplet runs in the *andante* part of her aria is an important trailer for one of the elements in the music of the Epilogue.

The 'dissolve' music leads to the fourth and final charade scene – some sort of trial. A strange jaunty little march (for trumpet and percussion) accompanies the arrival of Mangus–Prospero as judge and Faber–Ferdinand as jailer. Dov–Ariel is brought on in handcuffs. The report is:

> He's gone off his food.
> His wings are drooping.
> He used to sing before.

Mangus–Prospero grants him his liberty. 'That was fine, father', says Flora–Miranda, approvingly. Then Mel–Caliban is brought on in handcuffs to the same jaunty march. The report is:

> He sings alright;
> A pulsing, violent, sexy song.
> 'But he's a devil, a born devil.'
> You're better without him.

But in the end, thanks mainly to Flora–Miranda's intervention, Mel–Caliban gains his liberty too.

More or less total disintegration of the various layers of activity in the opera now sets in. Mangus–Prospero dismisses the charade and strides to the footlights. It is the finale. He no longer sings, but speaks direct to the audience.

> Enough! Enough!
> We look in the abyss.
> Lust for Caliban will not save us.
> Prospero's a fake, we all know that;
> And perhaps the Island's due to sink into the sea.
> Now that I break my staff and drown my book.

At this point a new musical sound is heard – voices singing in parts, 'Full fathom five, thy father lies.' In 1962 Tippett had written incidental music for a production of *The Tempest* at the Old Vic Theatre. Three *Songs for Ariel* were extracted that year and performed as a separate composition for voice and piano (or harpsichord). From these he now quoted fragments of 'Full fathom five' and 'Come unto these yellow sands', which are sung by Dov and one or two other singers, and echoed by spoken voices off-stage. All this is caught up in an ensemble – 'If for a timid moment we submit to love' – a quintet including all members of the cast, except Faber and Thea, who have moved aside.

This ensemble issues in departure. Mel goes with Denise. Flora follows by herself, radiant, dancing. Dov might wish to follow Flora but he cannot. A backward look from Mel draws him to follow Mel and Denise. Mangus disappears. Only Faber and Thea remain. The last of the 'dissolves' is an ascending one.

The Epilogue resumes the music of Thea's aria after the chess scene in the charade. At first she and Faber speak above the semi-quaver triplet runs now played by the celesta, but there are three striking passages for the two voices singing together in what sounds like still irreconcilable harmony: 'I encompass the vast night with an image of desire', 'Our enmity's transcended in desire', and 'The curtain rises'. And as the curtain literally falls, the orchestra elevates a surging foam of demisemiquavers from the lowest to the highest pitch level.

The Knot Garden was ready for production at an important moment in the fortunes of Covent Garden. Colin Davis, who had already shown himself to be an ideal interpreter of Tippett's music, had just been appointed musical director, and on his suggestion Peter Hall had been brought in as artistic director. Great things were expected of this duumvirate and one of the first operas on which the two directors collaborated was *The Knot Garden*. The production, which was distinguished by an imaginative setting of revolving aluminium rods devised by Timothy O'Brien, was a great success: both public and critics were delighted, and it seemed that the two directors were satisfied too. Unfortunately the partnership between Colin Davis and Peter Hall did not last long, Hall resigning in July 1971, but *The Knot Garden* enjoyed a run of six performances in December 1970 and was revived some two years later.

The Philips recording of the Covent Garden production conducted by Colin Davis was released early in 1974.

THE KNOT GARDEN

First performed 2 December 1970
Royal Opera House, Covent Garden

Opera in three acts.
Words and Music by Michael Tippett

FABER, *a civil engineer*	Raimund Herincx
THEA, *his wife, a gardener*	Yvonne Minton
FLORA, *their ward*	Jill Gomez
DENISE, *Thea's sister, a dedicated freedom fighter*	Josephine Barstow
MEL, *a negro writer*	Thomas Carey
DOV, *his white friend, a musician*	Robert Tear
MANGUS, *an analyst*	Thomas Hemsley
OFFSTAGE VOICES	

Conductor: Colin Davis
Producer: Peter Hall
Designed by Timothy O'Brien
Costumes by Tazeena Firth
Lighting by John Bury

6

Faces Behind the Masks
The Ice Break

In the previous chapter reference has been made to the *Songs for Dov*, which were completed just after the score of *The Knot Garden* was finished, and before its first performance. The first song was identical with Dov's strophic song at the end of Act II of the opera; but the other two were newly composed, both words and music.

In the second song Dov sings 'of the Wanderjahre, those years of illusion and disillusion, innocence and experience, which we all pass through to reach what maturity we may'. In his extended programme note to this song-cycle,* the composer emphasizes that this migratory movement is always to the west:

Ride off into the sunset.
I'm on my way.

For his second song he uses a verse and chorus form. The three verses each start with tiny relevant literary quotations. Thus: the first line of Mignon's song from Goethe's *Wilhelm Meister*, 'Kennst du das Land' and of Beethoven's setting; the first line of Ariel's song from *The Tempest*, 'Come unto these yellow sands', and of his own setting; the first line of the Sirens' song in Homer's *Odyssey*, with a musical quote from *King Priam*.

In the third song Dov journeys on a 'full circle west' across the tundra of Siberia back to the 'big town' where he was born. He is now a grown man, a creative artist struggling with the intractable problems of 'poets in a barren age'. He goes to look in on Zhivago and Lara in 'the forest hut where they had shacked up together'. But the two lovers themselves had gone away, back to the town, each alone into the swarming city. At this point Tippett wrote:

*from which I have quoted extensively.

For this Siberian journey in Song 3, I did not attempt to imitate the wonderful sense of great space in much Russian music. I could not have succeeded had I tried. But once 'in the town' I used a tiny hidden quotation from Mussorgsky, when Zhivago is found 'scribbling in an attic' the chronicles of his time.

There are moments when, of all the characters in Tippett's operas, Dov seems to be closest in temperament to the composer; and in some ways the references here to Siberia, Mussorgsky and *Boris Godunov*, to Pasternak and *Dr Zhivago* seem to hint at a new orientation of ideas which might reach fuller musical expression in the future. This indeed is what seems to have happened in *The Ice Break*.

It is often difficult to know where and when the initial impulse for the composition of a new work of art occurs. Sometimes the process may be set in motion by quite a tiny event. This is what seems to have happened when Tippett attended a performance of Berlioz's *Benvenuto Cellini* at Covent Garden, probably during the 1968-9 season, and was struck by the effect of the masked revellers in the Roman carnival scenes. It occurred to him that there was a significant distinction to be made between the anonymity of these revellers and their characterization as dramatis personae when not in Carnival disguise. When he came to plan *The Ice Break*, he realized that his action postulated the existence of several rival chorus groups and decided to insist on masking in some form or other, not only to enforce anonymity, but also to show that 'stereotypes are in question, rather than any presently exacerbated example'. The groups include the fans of a black athletics champion, and two masked or hooded choruses – one white (a kind of clan), the other black – whose tribal identities are established by ceremonial dancing.

In talking about *The Ice Break*, it is convenient to pretend that two specific parts of the world seem to be involved in its action, such as North America and Russia; but it is only fair to add that at no point in his libretto is Tippett explicit about locations or nationalities. Indeed, he goes to some pains to make it clear that, characteristically, he expects all the various aspects of his action to be subjected to some degree of surrealist interpretation.

In a note on the music, which prefaces the score, he wrote:

In the music there are two archetypal sounds; one related to the frightening but exhilarating sound of the ice breaking on the great northern rivers in the spring; the other related to the exciting or terrifying sound of the slogan-shouting crowds, which can lift you on their shoulders in triumph or stamp you to death.

'The sound of the ice breaking on the great northern rivers' presumably refers to the northward-flowing rivers in Siberia and elsewhere; and doubtless Tippett had still sounding in his mind Stravinsky's answer to Robert Craft's question 'What did you love most in Russia?' to which the composer of *The Rite of Spring* had replied:

The violent Russian spring that seemed to begin in an hour and was like the whole earth cracking. That was the most wonderful event of every year of my childhood.*

As for the sound of the slogan-shouting crowds in Act I, there is a group of young fans, some white, mostly black, who centre round Olympion, a black athletics champion; but in Act II the situation develops into mob rivalries between the Whites and Blacks. The white mob can be more or less equated with the Ku Klux Klan, as appears from its WASPish opening chorus:

A band of pure Caucasians,
The noblest of the klan,
We stand in rank together
White woman with white. . . .

The black mob's contribution is more ejaculatory:

Out, out, Whitey out, Whitey out.
Out, out, Whitey out, Whitey out,
Out, out, out, out, out, out.
Burn, baby, burn!
Burn, baby——

This gang warfare results in outbursts of hysterical violence, leading to casualties on both sides.

The framework for the action is postulated in the opening scene of Act I, which is set in a vast airport lounge-hall, where Nadia, an emigrant, who came to the country of her adoption twenty years ago with her baby boy, Yuri, is awaiting the arrival of her husband, Lev, who has just been released from prison in his native land and allowed to leave the country to rejoin his family. Lev arrives, and he and his wife are reunited, but there is a generation gap between father and

*Igor Stravinsky and Robert Craft, *Memories & Commentaries* (Faber & Faber, 1960).

son. Yuri's girl friend is Gayle, a white, but he disapproves of the
company she keeps – particularly the group of young blacks, who
idolise Olympion. This group includes Hannah, a black hospital
nurse, who is a close friend of Gayle's. (Perhaps Hannah is distantly
related to Claire, who was intended to have been a hospital doctor in
The Knot Garden, but was dropped from the cast list at the last moment.)

In Act II, the gang spirit that had been shown by Olympion's
followers in Act I develops into mob rivalries between the whites
and blacks. After the tribalization of the two sides there is a scene of
great violence on the stage, during which one of the masked figures
falls and is kicked to death. The melée ends in shooting.

In the last act Nadia dies of old age. She sings a 'swan song of
death' divided into three sections. The first, which is accompanied
by the 'metaphorical' sound of sleigh-bells, recalls her youth and
winter sleigh-rides in the forest with her brother and school friends.
The second recalls the bedroom where she slept as a child, and the
gentle music is suddenly interrupted by a strange splintering sound
'Ah – ee, ah – ee . . .' which denotes the noise of the ice breaking up
on one of the great northern rivers in spring. In the third section she
glides downstream in a tiny boat:

> The wide water is full of folk,
> Calling, calling. . . .

She dies, and Lev calls out: 'Nadia, Nadia, wait for me in Paradise.'

The word 'paradise' is the cue for a kind of enharmonic switch.
The scene changes from the setting for Nadia's death scene with its
metaphorical sound accompaniment to an imaginary 'Paradise
Garden'. This is the mid-point of Act III, and here the composer
indulges in a diversion or entertainment which he calls 'The Psychedelic Trip'. In the Garden, 'seekers of all kinds, tough and tender,
hippies, flower-people *et al.* are to be found, perhaps smoking pipes
of peace or pot'. From a black hole in the Universe, a psychedelic
messenger called Astron materialises. He has a double voice – that
is to say, the part is sung by lyric mezzo and high tenor (or counter
tenor) in virtual unison. The message he brings (a quotation from
Jung) is:

> Take care for the Earth.
> God will take care for himself.

and:

Spring come to you at the farthest
In the very end of harvest.

The chorus apostrophizes the visitor from outer space as, 'Messenger,' 'Angel,' 'Saviour,' 'Hero;' and Astron, in highly ironic tones rising to falsetto, repeats, 'Saviour?! Hero?! Me!!' adding in his natural voice, 'You must be joking.' Suddenly the image of Astron distintegrates, the Paradise Garden with the Chorus vanishes as if by explosion, and the freak-out is over.

What remains is the scene of Yuri's recovery and rebirth in hospital. The young man has been totally encased in plaster, and now the plaster carapace is cut away, his flesh reappearing dead-white. The finish of the operation is the signal for a brief irruption by the Chorus from the Paradise Garden, who whirl through the hospital like a carnival rout. Yuri is wheeled in from the operating theatre and takes his first tentative steps. The opera's final words (a quotation from Goethe) are given to his father:

Yet you will always be brought forth again,
glorious image of God,
and likewise be maimed, wounded afresh,
from within or without.

Tippett is one of the few composers of the twentieth century who has shown himself willing to tackle contemporary problems in his operas. This was certainly the case in *The Knot Garden*, where the problems were personal ones relating to a group of seven people, who happened to meet together in one place at one time. In *The Ice Break* emphasis is laid on contemporary difficulties of communication at various levels. The personal problem of Lev and Nadia hints at the implacable hostility of some ideological systems to free-thought or dissent. One of the problems of the generation gap is reflected in the relationship between Yuri and Lev. The racist problem of blacks and whites is highlit in the mob scenes, and this leads to the problem of reconciling the person seen as an individual with the same person acting as stereotype. Even the psychedelic trip, though it falls outside the main argument of the opera, may be said to illustrate an important aspect of the contemporary behaviour of the younger generation.

In *The Ice Break*, as in *The Midsummer Marriage* and *The Knot Garden*, Tippett has invented his own characters and action, and drafted his own libretto. He has also given a remarkable twist to his stage technique. There is no longer any question of using the Brechtian device of a commentary to join the various set scenes, as was the case in *King Priam*. Nor has he literally taken over the 'dissolve' device as used by him in *The Knot Garden*. His new technique is nearer to the needs of cinema and television than those of the theatre. In *The Ice Break* the massed use of the chorus has posed a number of problems for the producer, and the composer has given a clear indication of his intentions in the preliminary note to the vocal score and the libretto where he writes:

In a chorus scene the whole stage is occupied and any extant non-chorus scene totally submerged, even though when the chorus goes, the non-chorus scene appears once more still in progress.

This technique has enabled him to cut corners, delete inessentials, and move with great rapidity from scene to scene. The result was that *The Ice Break* became shorter even than *The Knot Garden* – a total length of 75 minutes instead of 87.

The 'totality' conception of the use of the stage means that in Act I the airport lounge-hall is omnipresent, but fades out for two intimate scenes between Nadia and Lev in Nadia's tiny apartment. Similarly in Act II the omnipresent scene is 'the city at night', which fades out twice to allow the audience's attention to concentrate on other intimate scenes in Nadia's apartment. In Act III the build-up is different. There are three sections to this act: the first is Nadia's death scene in her apartment; the second is the scene in the Paradise Garden, where the whole of the stage is opened up; and the third is Yuri's operation and recovery in a large hospital.

There are three main choral groups: in Act I Olympion's fans, mostly black, but some white; in Act II two rival, white-masked and black-masked choruses, the latter presumably including Olympion's fans; and in Act III, after the riot at the end of Act II, the rival mobs have disappeared and the members of their choruses appear as the flower children of the Paradise Garden. Olympion's fans are (to begin with) good-natured and noisy. They sing nonsense words – 'Ola, Olo' – to a rather spiky tune. But when Olympion arrives in triumph, their song and dance are found to prelude a bombastic air for Olympion – 'I'm beautiful: I'm black: I am unbeatable' – whose vocal line is embellished by florid decoration, melismata and occasional outbreaks of hocketing. As Olympion's boastfulness rises to a climax, Gayle is moved by the fervour of the black mob and, to Yuri's consternation, breaks in with her own impassioned utterance, in which she recalls how Olympion's

> people have lived this land
> as long as mine . . .
> but not in freedom: not as equals.

She offers to make amends; and as she goes down on her knees before Olympion, her hair seems to cover his feet. This is too much for Yuri. He attacks Olympion, but the champion knocks him down and kicks Gayle off with a single clean movement of his foot. Common-time foursquare metres and bar-groupings characterize Olympion's musical utterances and those of his followers with their shouted refrain of, 'Out, out, Whitey out;' but Gayle's more sophisticated nature is reflected in compound metres and groupings such as 2+3 and 2+3+2.

In Act II the rival mobs prepare themselves for action. Their assembly call, sounding like trumpets blown *forte* in the far distance, wails out over the city. As in a ritual, Gayle and Yuri put on their hoods and join the masked white chorus, which sings a stiff, insensitive, Methodist hymn tune:

> We meet with cordial greetings
> In this our sacred cave
> To pledge anew our compact
> With hearts sincere and brave.

The black masked chorus, when it arrives, produces a new, deadly refrain, 'Our fist, our boot, our hammer,' which alternates with cries of, 'Out, out,' and, 'Burn, baby, burn.' There is a momentary respite when the rival mobs leave the stage and then, after a gentle *pianissimo* instrumental prelude, Hannah sings her magnificent air 'Blue night of my soul'. This is the heart of the opera.

When the two masked mobs reappear on stage, they are supposed to enact the process of tribalization. Musically this consists of a medley formed by a series of instrumental confrontations which are being constantly varied and altered to accompany the tribal dancing. The following sections may be distinguished:

A   A cocky little passage for solo violin marked *brillante marcatissimo* with plentiful double-stopping.

B   A theme for solo clarinet marked *brillante: accenti forti*.

C   A heavy march-like passage for violins accompanied by remainder strings, marked *pesante* and *non legato*.

D   A theme, closely related to B, but turned into a two-part invention for (i) piccolos and (ii) oboes and cor anglais, with an accompaniment for five tuned drums and piano,* in which the metrical pattern is constantly varied.

E   A variant of C.

F   A slight variant of D.

G   A two-part invention consisting of A with a second part added for viola solo.

H   A two-part invention derived from D and F.

J   A further variant of C.

K   A further variant of B.

After the exposition of these restless short passages, the chorus enters the stage and the music builds up into a series of wordless climaxes – 'Wa wa wa' and 'b, b, b, b, b' – accompanied by the jostling of the tribalization tunes and obsessive drumming from the five tuned drums. This scene is temporarily broken to show Lev and Nadia in their apartment, muttering in a kind of cat's cradle of half-conscious thoughts. There is a sudden return to the all-over scene of the city at night. And now 'the black mob have someone from the white mob on the ground, writhing and crawling, and are kicking him to death. Each entry of the boot proceeds with a heavy thud and scream.' When the police car and ambulance arrive and the moment of unmasking comes, it is Olympion who has been shot by the whites, Gayle who has been kicked to death by the blacks, and Yuri who has been badly wounded.

After those violent and inhumane scenes it seems essential that the act should end with a moment of compassion and repose. And so it does. When the police car and ambulance have gone off with their sirens wailing into the distance, Lev and Hannah are left alone, on the stage seeking comfort in their sorrow. Nothing is sung. Instead, the orchestra provides a quiet instrumental postlude in the rhythm

---

*In a preliminary note on performance, the composer wrote: 'The five tuned drums in Act II (no others are used in that act) will probably be a group of pre-set timpani and/or might be called tuned tom-toms. Since the speed for the drummer is very fast indeed, the piano doubles every drum note without exception. It will not matter, therefore, if the drummer leaves notes unplayed occasionally if that alone enables the necessary speed to be reached.'

of a lullaby with solo parts for violin and cello accompanied by electric guitar and bass guitar with muted horns in the background.

After Act II, the black and white choruses have no further part to play as such, and their choristers are merged with the 'seekers of all kinds, tough and tender, past, present and future', who are in the Paradise Garden. None of the choruses in this opera is polyphonic in the sense that the big choruses in *The Midsummer Marriage* were. In nearly every case they make their effect by rather simplistic devices. In compensation, however, the opera has two important vocal ensembles, each consisting of a quartet of solo voices, which merit special attention.

At the beginning of Act II, Lev, Nadia, Yuri and Gayle are together, each in his or her private world and cut off from the others. Without preliminaries they plunge into a piece of tight four-part counterpoint, where each part is independent and each voice is buttressed by an orchestral instrument playing in unison with it – a favourite device in this opera score. After the first statement of the piece of knotted counterpoint, Lev, Yuri and Nadia break out of the ensemble for a brief snatch of dialogue. Then the contrapuntal refrain is resumed as before, and next time it is Gayle who breaks out of the ensemble, singing prophetically, 'Burn, baby, burn! What does that mean? that I be killed? . . . .'

The other quartet occurs towards the end of Act III, when Luke, Hannah and Yuri are within the operating theatre, while Lev is left to wait alone in the hall of the hospital, and all four of them are concentrating on the successful outcome (or otherwise) of Yuri's operation. Here the question of vocal balance is important; and from a preliminary note in the score the composer makes it clear that he is conscious that the voices of Luke, Hannah and Yuri may need amplification. This is no static quartet, but a running *scena* to which each of the singers contributes as and when he or she has cause.

When Tippett planned this opera, he must have been conscious of the fact that it had an inherent weakness in that, of its six main characters, two are killed in Act II, and a third is dangerously wounded. In addition, old age begins to take its toll. At the beginning of Act III, when Nadia is dozing in her apartment, Lev sits beside her, reading, Luke and Hannah call on her, and Nadia recalls various episodes from the days of her youth as she begins to sing her swan song of death. As she does so, her character becomes fuller and rounder, and this has an effect on the character of Lev as her former lover and present husband. By the time she dies, she and Lev have completely won the audience's interest, while Yuri, never a very firmly established character, recedes into a limbo between life and death, from which he may recover if his operation is successful, but that will be another song or another story. In fact, Yuri does not come well out of the opera and does not excite real sympathy. Judgement is suspended.

Sometimes Tippett's opera scores wash up strange bits of flotsam. In *The Ice Break* there is a moment fourteen bars before the final curtain, where over a fermata chord for electric organ the composer (quoting from Tennyson's *The Princess*) has written: 'as though in the far distance "the horns of elfland faintly blowing".'

One recognizes in this opera as well as in some of his other scores how hauntingly beautiful is Tippett's writing for horns.

In the course of this chapter, it has been made clear that *The Ice Break* represents a further stage in the condensation of Tippett's opera scores, an overall length of 75 minutes instead of 87 minutes for *The Knot Garden*. Here is a table, in minutes, based on the timing of actual performances that covers all four of them and shows how drastic has been the movement towards compression and economy in the thirty or so years of his operatic activity:

	ACT I	ACT II	ACT III	TOTAL
The Midsummer Marriage	60	31	59	150
King Priam	42	24	50	116
The Knot Garden	31	23	33	87
The Ice Break	22	25	28	75

When the time came to arrange the production of *The Ice Break* at the Royal Opera House, Covent Garden, which had commissioned the work, Peter Hall was no longer available as producer, having been recently appointed director of the National Theatre, so the choice fell on Sam Wanamaker, who had made such a success of *King Priam* fifteen years previously. He had the advantage of being American, so racial discord was a familiar issue to him. He was also able to exercise a guiding hand over some of the colloquialisms in Tippett's text. Scenery and costumes were by Ralph Koltai, whose open-plan setting suited the opera and made it possible for the action to change at lightning speed (though not always noiselessly) from the full-stage airport lounge-hall or the city at night, to Nadia's small apartment room. The movements in the mob scenes and in the tribal dances were supervised by choreographer Walter Raines. Lighting was in the hands of David Hersey and included interesting laser-beam effects in the Paradise Garden. The first performance (7 July 1977) was conducted by Colin Davis, to whom the opera was dedicated.

The first production abroad came the following year. *Wenn das Eis bricht* was given at the Opernhaus, Kiel (26 June 1978), in a German translation by Ken W. Bartlett. The music direction was in the hands of Walter Gillessen and the producer was Heinz Lukas-Kindermann. The cast was a young and talented one and the younger members of the audience showed especial interest and enthusiasm. This was followed within a year by a production by the Opera Company of Boston, Massachusetts, directed by Sarah Caldwell (18 May 1979). Here too the audience was captivated.

THE ICE BREAK

First performed 7 July 1977
Royal Opera House, Covent Garden

Opera in three acts.
Words and Music by Michael Tippett

LEV*, *50-year-old teacher; released after twenty years prison and exile*	John Shirley-Quirk
NADIA, *his wife; who emigrated with their baby son*	Heather Harper
YURI, *their son; a student and second-generation immigrant*	Tom McDonnell
GAYLE, *Yuri's present and native-born white girl friend*	Josephine Barstow
HANNAH, *Gayle's black friend; a hospital nurse*	Beverly Vaughn
OLYMPION, *Hannah's boy friend; a black champion*	Clyde Walker
LIEUTENANT, *A lieutenant of Police*	Roderick Kennedy
LUKE, *a young intern at Hannah's hospital*	John Dobson
ASTRON†, *a psychedelic messenger*	Anne Wilkens
	James Bowman

CHORUS, EXTRA CHORUS *and*
DANCERS: *airport personnel and
passengers; fans and associates of
Olympion; Black and White mobs,
'seekers' in the Paradise Garden;
hospital staff and patients*

Conductor: Colin Davis
Producer: Sam Wanamaker
Scenery and costumes by Ralph Koltai
Choreography by Walter Raines
Lighting by David Hersey

*Lev sings through an off-stage microphone some scenes before he appears.

†Astron (two voices) sings through an off-stage microphone and only appears as a laser officer (no actual body on stage).

7
Coda

It is tempting to speculate what might have happened had T. S. Eliot responded positively to Tippett's request for a libretto for his oratorio, *A Child of Our Time*. It seems likely that whatever text Eliot might have written himself, or recommended, would have been accepted by the composer; and so, when in the course of time there was question of composing an opera instead of an oratorio, there would have been a strong likelihood of the same team being used again. Of Eliot's extant verse plays the one that seems closest in content and style to the type of fable Tippett eventually evolved for some of his operas is *The Family Reunion*; but it is always possible that the two men might have found a basis for collaboration that would have resulted in a new text or texts. It is also possible that Tippett might have been tempted to work with another congenial writer, such as Christopher Fry. But once Eliot had suggested that Tippett's original draft sketch for the libretto for *A Child of Our Time* could stand on its own after a certain degree of revision and titivation, the die was cast; and when the time came Tippett decided to assume responsibility for his future opera librettos himself.

As can be seen from the correspondence reprinted in Chapter 3, the libretto for *The Midsummer Marriage* evolved over a period which included the time it took him to compose the score. It is therefore hardly surprising that it reveals certain tentative elements. But how beneficial was his experience with *The Midsummer Marriage* can be seen as soon as one comes to the following opera, for the libretto for *King Priam* gives an impression of complete professional mastery. It is true that here the composer has possibly been aided by the preliminary decision to base the opera on familiar characters and action as commemorated in the *Iliad*. If he had stuck to this formula – of dealing with operatic adaptations of material drawn from well-known myths, his position as an opera composer would have been close to that of Richard Wagner; but he chose to exercise his right as a creative artist to insist on complete control of his operatic material, and for his subsequent operas (*The Knot Garden* and *The Ice Break*) he reverted to his original aim of creating the characters and inventing the action as well as writing the librettos.

Each of his four operas has taken him, on average, about seven years to invent, plan, draft and compose. This represents operatic control by the composer of a rare degree of intensity and comprehensiveness. Such coverage by a single individual is virtually unique in the annals of opera, where most of the established works are the result of the sort of collaboration in which, with the approval of the composer, a librettist produces a text which is related to an original play, poem or story. Here composer and librettist are one; and the result is that the librettos are as closely tailored to the composer's needs and wishes as is humanly possible. In fact, it is clear from Tippett's last two operas that one of the results of this unified control has been to cut verbal luxuriance to a minimum, thereby shortening the actual time taken in performance and giving the audience a succession of comparatively short, but extremely concentrated, operatic scenes.

Prose, or free verse, is now the preferred medium.

It is difficult to prophesy the effect of all this on the future of English opera, or on the future of opera in general; but it is now clear that Tippett's operatic contribution is a unique one, and that the growing acceptance of his operas – particularly in the English-speaking world of Great Britain, North America and Australia – is likely to have important repercussions on operatic developments in the future.

Appendix
Chronological List of Published Compositions
COMPILED BY ALAN WOOLGAR

1934/5 **String Quartet No. 1** revised 1943
'To Wilfred Franks'.
First performed by the Brosa Quartet at a Lemare Concert, Mercury Theatre, London, December 1935: revised version by the Zorian Quartet, Wigmore Hall, London, February 1944. (In the revised version, a new first movement replaces the original first and second movements.)

1936/7 **Sonata for Piano** revised 1942 and 1954
'To Francesca Allinson'.
First performed by Phyllis Sellick, Queen Mary Hall, London, November 1938. (In the revised version, the original 5th variation of the first movement is shortened.)

1938/9 **Concerto for Double String Orchestra**
'To Jeffrey Mark'.
First performed by the South London Orchestra conducted by the composer, Morley College, London, April 1940.

1939/41 **Fantasia on a Theme of Handel** for Piano and Orchestra
'To Phyllis Sellick'.
First performed by Phyllis Sellick and the Walter Goehr Orchestra conducted by Walter Goehr, Wigmore Hall, March 1942. (The theme is taken from the Prelude to the Air with Variations in Handel's Suites de pièces pour le clavecin', Vol. 2 (*c.* 1733), as quoted by Samuel Butler in *Erewhon*.)

1939/41 A Child of Our Time Oratorio for SATB soloists, chorus and orchestra, with text by the composer.

First performed by Joan Cross, Margaret McArthur, Peter Pears, Roderick Lloyd, London Region Civil Defence Choir and Morley College Choir and the London Philharmonic Orchestra conducted by Walter Goehr, Adelphi Theatre, London, March 1944.

1941/42 String Quartet No. 2 in F sharp
'To Walter Bergmann'.
First performed by the Zorian Quartet, Wigmore Hall, March 1943.

1942 Two Madrigals for unaccompanied chorus SATB:
The Windhover (poem by Gerard Manley Hopkins).
The Source (poem by Edward Thomas).
'To Morley College Choir'.
First performed by the Morley College Choir conducted by Walter Bergmann, Morley College, July 1943.

1943 Boyhood's End Cantata on a text by W. H. Hudson for tenor and piano
'To Peter Pears and Benjamin Britten'.
First performed by Peter Pears and Benjamin Britten, Morley College, June 1943.

1943 Fanfare No. 1 for 4 horns, 3 trumpets and 3 trombones
Written for the 50th anniversary of the consecration of St Matthew's Church, Northampton.
First performed, September 1943.

1943 Plebs Angelica motet for double chorus
'For the choir of Canterbury Cathedral, January 1944'.
Commissioned by Canterbury Cathedral. First performed by the Fleet Street Choir conducted by T. B. Lawrence, Canterbury Cathedral, September 1944.

1944 The Weeping Babe motet for soprano solo and unaccompanied chorus SATB (poem by Edith Sitwell)
'In memory of Bronwen Wilson, August 8th 1944'.
Commissioned by the BBC for 'Poet's Christmas' 1944. First per-

formed by Margaret Ritchie and Morley College Choir conducted by the composer, The Polytechnic, Regent Street, London, December 1944.

1944/5 Symphony No. 1

First performed by the Liverpool Philharmonic Orchestra conducted by Malcolm Sargent, Philharmonic Hall, Liverpool, November 1945.

1945/6 String Quartet No. 3

'To Mrs Mary Behrend'
Commissioned by Mary Behrend. First performed by the Zorian Quartet, Wigmore Hall, October 1946.

1946 Preludio Al Vespro di Monteverdi for organ

'For Geraint Jones'
Written to precede a performance of Monteverdi's *Vespers* 1610, Central Hall, Westminster, November 1946; first performed by Geraint Jones. (A fragment of the plainsong melody *Sancta Maria* and the whole melody of *Ave Maris Stella* are used as material for the Prelude).

1946 Little Music for string orchestra

'For the 10th anniversary of the Jacques String Orchestra'.
First performed by the Jacques Orchestra conducted by Reginald Jacques, Wigmore Hall, November 1946.

1946/52 The Midsummer Marriage opera in 3 acts with text by the composer

First performed by the Covent Garden Opera, conducted by John Pritchard, produced by Christopher West, with scenery and costumes by Barbara Hepworth and choreography by John Cranko, Royal Opera House, Covent Garden, January 1955.

Ritual Dances from The Midsummer Marriage for orchestra with optional chorus

'To Walter Goehr'.
First performed by the Basel Kammerorchester conducted by Paul Sacher, Basel, February 1953.

1948 Suite for the Birthday of Prince Charles (Suite in D)

Commissioned by the BBC in celebration of the birth of Prince Charles. First performed by the BBC Symphony Orchestra conducted by Sir Adrian Boult, November 1948. (The first movement is a chorale prelude on the hymn tune 'Crimond'; the second uses a traditional French melody; the third the march from Act 1 of *The Midsummer Marriage* and an Irish version of 'All round my hat'; the fourth the English medieval hymn 'Angelus ad Virginem'; and the last 'Early one morning', the Helston Furry Dance, a 'folk' tune of the composer's and material re-worked from the overture to *Robin Hood*.)

1950/1 The Heart's Assurance song-cycle for high voice and piano (poems by Sydney Keyes and Alun Lewis)

'In memory of Francesca Allinson (1902-1945)'.
Commissioned by Peter Pears. First performed by Peter Pears and Benjamin Britten, Wigmore Hall, May 1951.

1952 Dance Clarion Air Madrigal for five voices SSATB with text by Christopher Fry

From the collection of songs for mixed voices, A Garland for the Queen, commissioned by the Arts Council of Great Britain to mark the occasion of the Coronation of Her Majesty Queen Elizabeth II, of which the composers were Bax, Berkeley, Bliss, Finzi, Howells, Ireland, Rawsthorne, Rubbra, Tippett & Vaughan Williams. First performed by the Golden Age Singers and the Cambridge University Madrigal Society conducted by Boris Ord, Royal Festival Hall, London, June 1953.

1953 Fanfare No. 2 for 4 trumpets
1953 Fanfare No. 3 for 3 trumpets
Written for the St Ives Festival of Arts, June 1953.

1953 Fantasia Concertante on a Theme of Corelli for string orchestra

Commissioned by the Edinburgh Festival 1953, in celebration of the tercentenary of the birth of Arcangelo Corelli. First performed by the BBC Symphony Orchestra conducted by the composer, Usher Hall,

Edinburgh, August 1953. (The theme is taken from the *Adagio/Vivace* section from the first movement of Corelli's Concerto Grosso in F, Op. 6, No. 2).

1953/4 Divertimento on 'Sellinger's Round' for Chamber Orchestra

'Dedicated to Paul Sacher'. Commissioned by Paul Sacher. First performed by the Collegium Musicum Zurich conducted by Paul Sacher, Zurich, November 1954. (A variation of the traditional tune 'Sellinger's Round' appears in all five movements. Incorporated in the movements are quotations from a Gibbons Fantasia, Dido's first song in Purcell's *Dido and Aeneas,* the song 'Preach me not your musty rules' from the Masque in *Comus* by Thomas Arne, Nocturne in D minor for piano by John Field and 'I have a song to sing' from *The Yeomen of the Guard* by Arthur Sullivan. The second movement was written for the Aldeburgh Festival 1953 as part of a composite work, *Variations on an Elizabethan Theme,* of which the other five movements were written by Lennox Berkeley, Benjamin Britten, Arthur Oldham, Humphrey Searle and William Walton.)

1953/5 Concerto for Piano and Orchestra
'To Evelyn Maude'.
Commissioned by the City of Birmingham Symphony Orchestra in conjunction with the John Feeney Charitable Trust. First performed by Louis Kentner and the City of Birmingham Symphony Orchestra conducted by Rudolf Schwarz, Town Hall, Birmingham, October 1956.

1954 Four Inventions for descant and treble recorders
Written for the Society of Recorder Players. First performed by Freda Dinn and Walter Bergmann, Society of Recorder Players' Summer School, Roehampton, July 1954.

1955 Sonata for Four Horns
First performed by the Dennis Brain Wind Ensemble, Wigmore Hall, December 1955.

1956 Bonny at Morn Northumbrian folk song set for unison voices and recorders (two descants and treble)

Written for the 10th birthday of the International Pestalozzi Children's Village at Trogen (Switzerland). First performed, April 1956.

1956 Four Songs from the British Isles for unaccompanied chorus SATB
1. England 'Early one morning' 2. Ireland 'Lilliburlero' 3. Scotland 'Poortith cauld' 4. Wales 'Gwenllian'.

Commissioned by the Nordwestdeutschland Sangerbund, Bremen. First performed by the London Bach Group conducted by John Minchinton, Royaumont Festival (France), July 1958.

1956/7 Symphony No. 2
'To John Minchinton'.
Commissioned by the BBC First performed by the BBC Symphony Orchestra conducted by Sir Adrian Boult, Royal Festival Hall, February 1958.

1958 Crown of the Year Cantata with text by Christopher Fry for chorus SSA, recorders or flutes, oboe, cornet or trumpet, string quartet, percussion, handbells and piano

Commissioned by Eric Walter White for the centenary celebrations at Badminton School, Bristol. First performed under the composer's direction, July 1958. The instrumental Preludes in this cantata contain settings of 'O Mistress Mine', 'Marlborough s'en va-t-en guerre', the Austrian canon 'O wie wohl ist mir am Abend' and the American folk ballad 'Frankie and Johnny'.

1958 Wadhurst Hymn Tune (Unto the hills around do I lift up my longing eyes)
Written for the Salvation Army.

1958 Five Negro Spirituals from *A Child of Our Time* arranged for unaccompanied chorus
1. Steal away 2. Nobody knows 3. Go down, Moses 4. By and by 5. Deep river.

1958/61 King Priam opera in 3 acts with text by the composer
'To Karl Hawker'.

Written for the Koussevitsky Foundation in memory of Mrs Natalie Koussevitsky. First performed by the Covent Garden Opera conducted by John Pritchard, produced by Sam Wanamaker and with scenery and costumes by Sean Kenny, Coventry Theatre, Coventry, May 1962 (Coventry Cathedral Festival).

1960 **Music** Unison Song (poem by Shelley) for voices, strings and piano, or voices and piano
Written for the Jubilee of the East Sussex and West Kent Choral Festival, 1960. First performed by the combined choirs of the East Sussex and West Kent Choral Festival conducted by Trevor Harvey, Assembly Hall, Tunbridge Wells, April 1960.

1960 **Words for Music Perhaps** Incidental music for speaking voices and chamber ensemble to a sequence of poems by W. B. Yeats
Commissioned by the BBC. First broadcast, June 1960.

1960 **Lullaby** for six voices, or alto solo (or counter-tenor) and small choir SSTTB (poem by W. B. Yeats)
Written for the 10th birthday of the Deller Consort. First performed by the Deller Consort, Victoria and Albert Museum, London, November 1960.

1961 **Songs for Achilles** for tenor and guitar with texts by the composer
1. 'In the Tent' 2. 'Across the Plain' 3. 'By the Sea'
First performed by Peter Pears and Julian Bream, Aldeburgh Festival, June 1961. (The first song appears in Act 2 of *King Priam*.)

1961 **Magnificat and Nunc Dimittis** for chorus SATB and organ (Collegium Sancti Johannis Cantabrigiense)
Composed for the 450th anniversary of the foundation of St John's College, Cambridge, 1961. First performed by the St John's College Chapel Choir conducted by George Guest, March 1962.

1962 **Sonata No. 2 for Piano**
'To Margaret Kitchin, with affection and esteem'.

First performed by Margaret Kitchin, Freemason's Hall, Edinburgh Festival, September 1962. (Motifs from Act 2 of *King Priam* appear in this Sonata.)

1962 Songs for Ariel for voice and piano (or harpsichord)

1. 'Come unto these yellow sands' 2. 'Full fathom five' 3. 'Where the bee sucks'

First performed by Grayston Burgess and Virginia Pleasants at Fenton House, Hampstead, September 1963. (Adapted from incidental music written for a production of Shakespeare's *The Tempest*, Old Vic Theatre, London, April 1962. The Songs were arranged in 1964 for an instrumental accompaniment of flute/piccolo, clarinet, horn, percussion ad lib. (bells, bass drum) and harpsichord.

1962 Praeludium for Brass, Bells and Percussion

Commissioned for the 40th anniversary of the BBC. First performed by BBC Symphony Orchestra conducted by Antal Dorati, Royal Festival Hall, November 1962.

1962/3 Concerto for Orchestra

'To Benjamin Britten with affection and admiration in the year of his 50th birthday'.
Commissioned for the Edinburgh Festival 1963. First performed by the London Symphony Orchestra conducted by Colin Davis, Usher Hall, Edinburgh, August 1963. (Motifs from Acts 2 and 3 of *King Priam* appear in the finale.)

1963 Prelude, Recitative and Aria for flute, oboe and piano (or harpsichord)

First performed by the Oriana Trio on the BBC, February 1964. (Arrangement of the third interlude in Act 3 of *King Priam*.)

1963/5 The Vision of Saint Augustine for baritone solo, chorus and orchestra

'Matri, patrisque in memoriam'.
Commissioned by the BBC. First performed by Dietrich Fischer-Dieskau and the BBC Symphony Orchestra conducted by the composer at the Royal Festival Hall, January 1966.

1965/70 The Shires Suite for chorus and orchestra

This Suite was written during this period for the Leicestershire Schools Symphony Orchestra and consists of the following five movements:

Prologue for chorus and orchestra (1965)
Interlude 1 for orchestra (1970)
Cantata for chorus and orchestra (1970)
Interlude 2 for orchestra (1969)
Epilogue for chorus and orchestra (1965)

First complete performance by the Schola Cantorum of Oxford and the Leicestershire Schools Symphony Orchestra conducted by the composer, Cheltenham Festival, July 1970.

1966 Severn Bridge Variations No. 6 'Braint'. Variations on a traditional Welsh melody (unpublished)

Commissioned by the BBC West Region. First performed by the BBC Training Orchestra conducted by Sir Adrian Boult, Brangwyn Hall, Swansea, January 1967. (A composite work by Arnold, Hoddinott, Maw, Daniel Jones, Grace Williams, Tippett to commemorate the first birthday of the BBC Training Orchestra, its first visit to Wales, and of the opening of the Severn Bridge.)

1970 Songs for Dov for tenor and small orchestra with text by the composer

'To Eric Walter White'.
Commissioned by the Music Department, University College, Cardiff with assistance from the Welsh Arts Council. First performed by Gerald English and the London Sinfonietta conducted by the composer, University College, Cardiff, October 1970. (The first song appears in Act 2 of *The Knot Garden*.)

1966/70 The Knot Garden opera in 3 acts with text by the composer

'To Sir David Webster of the Royal Opera House, Covent Garden'.
Commissioned by the Royal Opera House, Covent Garden. First performed by the Covent Garden Opera conducted by Colin Davis, produced by Peter Hall, designed by Timothy O'Brien and with costumes by Tazeena Firth, Royal Opera House, Covent Garden, December 1970.

1970/2 **Symphony No. 3** for soprano and orchestra with text by the composer

'To Howard Hartog'.

Commissioned by the London Symphony Orchestra. First performed by Heather Harper with the London Symphony Orchestra conducted by Colin Davis, Royal Festival Hall, June 1972.

1971 **In Memoriam Magistri** for flute, clarinet and string quartet

Commissioned by *Tempo* magazine in memory of Igor Stravinsky. First performed by the London Sinfonietta, June 1972.

1972/3 **Sonata No. 3 for Piano**

'To Anna Kallin'.

Commissioned by Paul Crossley. First performed by Paul Crossley, Bath Festival, May 1973.

1973/6 **The Ice Break** opera in 3 acts with text by the composer

'To Colin Davis'.

Commissioned by the Royal Opera House, Covent Garden. First performed by Covent Garden Opera, conducted by Colin Davis, produced by Sam Wanamaker, with scenery and costumes by Ralph Koltai, Royal Opera House, Covent Garden, July 1977.

1976/7 **Symphony No. 4**

'To Ian Kemp'.

Commissioned by the Chicago Symphony Orchestra. First performed by the Chicago Symphony Orchestra conducted by Sir Georg Solti, Chicago, October 1977.

1977/8 **String Quartet no. 4**

'To Michael Tillett'.

First performed by the Lindsay Quartet, Bath Festival, May 1979.

1978/9 **Triple Concerto** for Violin, Viola, Cello and Orchestra

Index

INDEX